LOUIS XIV
and his world

RAGNHILD HATTON

LOUIS XIV

and his world

THAMES AND HUDSON
LONDON

Frontispiece: Absolutism personified.
Bust of Louis XIV, by Coysevox.

*Printed in Great Britain by Jarrold and
Sons Ltd, Norwich*

ISBN 0 500 13039 6

PREFACE

In history myth-making plays a significant role, but it is the task of the professional historian to evaluate the myth without falling under its spell. The origins
of historical myths are interesting in themselves and must be searched for. In
Louis XIV's case we come across a variety of myths. Some, such as that of the
ruler whose power was absolute, were fabricated by Louis himself and by
those who served him in the hope of fostering unity and reforms in France;
others, such as that of an ever aggressive Louis bent on bringing about a second
Counter-Reformation and Universal Monarchy in Europe, were woven by
those oligarchically governed states of the Protestant faith who found themselves
at war with Louis' France: the epithet 'the Christian Turk', used in the propaganda pamphlets of the period, can be explained by the hatred and fear which
the English and the Dutch felt for the French absolutist form of government.
Historians have added myths of their own, often in attempts at interpretation
before sufficient facts were at their disposal; and popular historians have relied
so heavily on the readily accessible sources (printed memoirs, diaries and
letters) as to distort the role of Louis as head of the French state.

Interest in the intellectual and artistic aspects of the *Grand Siècle* has always
been strong, and scholarly studies in these fields have long been available. In
recent years hard slogging work in the archives by many scholars has produced
results which enable us to see Louis XIV in deeper perspective. We have, for
instance, gained new insight into the financial and administrative history of the
reign, we know the way the censorship worked, what popular culture was like,
how the symbolism of the Sun-King developed – and though there are still
gaps, especially in local provincial studies, in biographies of important ministers and in the periods of diplomatic history of the reign, we possess enough
case-studies to permit us to generalize with a fair amount of certainty.

This book is intended for the general reader and has therefore no scholarly
apparatus, but I have planned the index in such a way that persons and themes
touched upon in the text and in the captions are explained. Experts will realize,
and the last section of the brief bibliography will indicate, my debt to the many
French, American and English scholars at present working on various aspects
of the reign of Louis XIV. As space forbids individual mention, they are
hereby collectively thanked. I wish to record my appreciation that the pub-
lishers permitted me to hunt for and choose the illustrations for the book and
the pleasure I found in working with Stanley Baron and Constance Kaine in
the layout of them. The illustrations and the map are an integral part of my
attempt to depict Louis and his world.

Louis, the fourteenth king of France of this name, was born on 5 September 1638 at Saint-Germain-en-Laye, not in the large château built there by François I but in a small brick building – within the château complex – constructed by his own paternal grandfather, Henri IV, and termed a pleasure house. France was then at war, having entered the religio-political struggle which had raged in Europe since 1618 (known to posterity as the Thirty Years War) by declaring war on Spain in 1635. The consequences of this coloured Louis' infancy and childhood and influenced his mature attitude towards politics, domestic and foreign, in important ways.

Weighty reasons had prompted both France's delay in joining openly in the fray and the eventual entry on the Protestant side. Since the very outbreak of the war, which ranged the Austrian and Spanish Habsburg states and most Catholic German princes against the German Protestant princes and their Scandinavian allies, France had played an indirect part on the anti-Habsburg side. Spain was a mighty neighbour, rich in territory, with gold and silver from her overseas empire in seemingly inexhaustible quantities, and an army possessed of a deservedly high reputation. Moreover, she was in a manner encircling France. An earlier French king, Charles VIII, had in 1494 sacrificed the gap in the Pyrenees (that is, the provinces of Cerdagne and Roussillon) to Spain in the hope – mistaken as it turned out – that he would be given a free hand in his invasion of Italy. Spain's victory in the long drawn-out Italian wars meant that by 1559 Sicily, Naples and most Tuscan ports (the so-called *presidii*) formed part of the Spanish state while the duchy of Milan had become the personal possession of the Spanish king. The Balearic islands, and Spain's Mediterranean galley fleet, facilitated transport of troops to northern Italy and from there to those territories on France's eastern border which had come to Spain by inheritance from the old Burgundian state: Franche-Comté, Luxembourg and the Netherlands. In 1609 the Northern Netherlands had forced Spain to agree to an eleven years' truce in that struggle which had broken out in the 1560s for local autonomy and developed into a fight for independence; and it looked as if the Dutch – led by good commanders of the House of Orange – would be able to maintain their independence as 'the Dutch Republic'* even after the war with Spain had reopened in 1621 and merged with the Thirty Years War. The Southern Netherlands (more vulnerable from the geographical and strategic points of view) had, however, returned to Spanish

* Also known as the United Provinces and sometimes as the States General after the diet or parliament to which the seven federated provinces sent representatives.

Opposite: The line of descent. Medal showing Louis' grandparents, Henri IV and Marie de Médicis, with his father, Louis XIII, as an infant. By Guillaume Dupré.

overrule on receiving confirmation of their local rights and now sheltered the pick of the Spanish army. On her northern frontier France was thus particularly vulnerable, the water-courses of the Meuse, the Lys and the Scheldt favouring Spain. Paris, it had long been realized, was so situated as to be without natural lines of defence, and in 1636 the Spaniards captured and held for a year Corbie, some 70 miles north of Paris; during the war period (which lasted till 1659) France suffered more than a dozen invasions from the north and east.

The division of the vast Habsburg empire into a Spanish and an Austrian branch on Charles V's abdication in 1556 had been greeted with relief in French circles since this stripped Charles' son Philip of the power and prestige of his father in the Germanies. Philip II inherited Spain and all her possessions and also the duchy of Milan (formerly an Imperial fief); but the Austrian possessions, and the right to stand as the Habsburg candidate in elections for the Emperorship of the Holy Roman Empire of the German Nation, went to Charles V's younger brother Ferdinand and his heirs. Ferdinand added to the Austrian territories the Bohemian and Hungarian ones (the latter much reduced by the Ottoman advance of the 1520s) which he had inherited, and was known to be preoccupied with his own eastern frontier and its security against the Turks, content to leave the Empire more or less to its own devices. The danger of his making Austrian Habsburg power a reality in the Germanies receded and the 'iron ring round the heart of France' eased for a while.

Things changed, however, with the years. Indeed, the establishing of relatively good relations with the Ottoman Sultan, though at the cost of paying him tribute, enabled Ferdinand's heirs to return to an active policy in the Empire. Ferdinand of Styria, the Habsburg candidate for the next Imperial election, gave due warning in 1607 and 1608 that, if he became Emperor, he would fight Protestantism, whether Lutheran or Calvinist, and would no longer regard the Peace of Augsburg (1555) as binding. To support the Church of Rome and Habsburg interests he was prepared, and he made no secret of it, to intervene in the succession disputes for the rich Rhine duchies of Cleve, Jülich, Berg, Mark and Ravensberg when their old and childless Protestant ruler died.

Such a prospect was alarming for France. Not only did it run counter to the policy of co-existence among the three major churches, which Henri IV and his adviser Sully wished to foster, but the presence of Austrian Habsburg troops so close to the French eastern frontier would pose a grave political problem and endanger the enclaves inside German territory (the bishoprics of Metz, Toul and Verdun) which had come to France as the price paid by the German Protestant princes for much-needed French help against Charles V in the 1550s. Since that time Metz, Toul and Verdun had been administered as French possessions, protected by certain treaty rights though formal sovereignty had not been secured. Henri IV found the situation so menacing that he decided on war to keep the Rhine duchies out of Habsburg hands, or out of the hands of a Habsburg client-ruler. A war-chest was got together with help from the Dutch, equally fearful of Austrian Habsburg Catholic power so close to their own borders; an army was raised; and only Henri IV's assassination in 1610 by a French religious fanatic postponed the outbreak of the religio-political struggle in the Empire till 1618.

Henri's assassination posed problems at home. His only child, a boy named Louis, was only nine years old, and – as always during royal minorities – this played into the hands of the French great noble families – *les grands*. These resented the growing accumulation of power at the centre and argued that France was so large a country that the form of government best suited to her size was something on the lines of the German Empire: the king ought to be a figurehead, much as the Emperors were after 1555, and real power in the provinces ought to lie with the high nobility who should aim to achieve recognition as territorial princes. In the circumstances Henri's widow, named regent for the child-king, had to bribe the nobles into acquiescence by dividing the war-chest among the most restive and powerful ones. When Louis XIII was declared of age, the position – as always when a minority came to an end – improved; but the young King and the adviser who increasingly influenced him, the Cardinal Richelieu, had to keep a watchful eye on the high nobility all through the reign. Duels were forbidden, in order to teach subjects that they must take up arms only at the behest of the king. Fortifications of noble castles were prohibited, to discourage military defiance of central power. Quite a few duellists, however, had to be put to death and many fortifications had to be forcibly destroyed to inculcate even moderate obedience. Plots to topple Richelieu and gain the ear of the King – and sometimes to usurp the position of the King – punctuated the reign throughout the 1620s. So did attempts by French Protestants (the Huguenots), noble and bourgeois, to achieve – with foreign help when obtainable – independent 'cantons' inside France. They wished to take to their logical conclusions those guarantees for religious freedom which the Edict of Nantes had vouchsafed them in 1598, an edict reaffirmed on Henri IV's death, while the central power desired to restrict the liberties of the adherents of the R.P.R. (*Religion Prétendue Réformée*) as much as possible.

Richelieu, beset by difficulties at home, had to abandon his first intervention in the Thirty Years War – an attempt to control the Val Telline of the Graubünden (the Grisons League) so as to deny Spanish troops the vital passage from the Milanese to the German battlefields. From 1627 Spanish armies used the Val Telline route without hindrance, and Richelieu and Louis XIII had to restrict themselves to giving diplomatic and financial succour to the anti-Habsburg forces in the Empire; this they did in the hope of staving off a unitary *Monarchie* of the Austrian Habsburgs in the Germanies. Danish military help for the Protestant side, between 1625 and 1629, proved insufficient against such Habsburg commanders as the Spanish Netherlander Tilly and the Bohemian Wallenstein; and though King Gustavus Adolphus proved spectacularly successful the Swedes were, after his death, badly routed at Nördlingen in 1634 thanks, mainly, to the advent of 8,000 fresh Spanish troops coming up via the Val Telline pass. This defeat for the anti-Habsburg side made French military intervention essential, and the declaration of war against Philip IV in 1635 was followed by one in 1636 against the Austrian Habsburgs.

The war-situation and the tensions within France which it brought in its train affected the royal family. At the age of fourteen, Louis XIII had been married to the Spanish infanta Ana (Anne) – styled, as were all Spanish princes and princesses of the Habsburg House, 'of Austria' – who was exactly

his own age; their marriage was not consummated till they were eighteen. She was healthier, taller and stronger than her slight, rheumatic and tubercular husband, who did not take to her. He was sensitive and serious, intensely practical (he liked making things with his own hands at his work-bench and in his smithy), keen on hunting and an expert falconer. He found her at one and the same time too Spanish in her pride and insistence on ceremony and too frivolous in her amusements: she had a passion, which he did not share, for gambling; he liked early hours for supper and bed, she preferred late ones.

For years Louis XIII seemed indifferent to advisers and confessors reminding him of his duty to give France an heir of his own body. The Queen had conceived shortly after consummation of the marriage in 1618, but there was an early miscarriage, attributed to her having run a race with one of her ladies-in-waiting. A second pregnancy, in 1630, also resulted in miscarriage, and from that time onwards Louis XIII had avoided his wife's bed. Suspicions as to the Queen's loyalty to France and friction between Anne and Richelieu embittered the relations of the royal couple. Anne, who at her husband's request had sent home most of her Spanish entourage, carried on a clandestine correspondence with the country of her birth and was involved in various intrigues which, if not directly treacherous, ran counter to the policies of her husband and his chief minister. Rumours began to circulate of a coming divorce and of her being sent into a convent for life. At a critical moment the loyalty of her servants saved her: a lady-in-waiting got into the Bastille and gave instructions to La Porte, one of the Queen's servants, who had been arrested for carrying Anne's letters; he stuck to the story she gave him, even when threatened by torture, so that it might fit the answers Anne had given under interrogation. The Queen's position improved, 'miraculously' it was judged, when she became pregnant as a consequence of the King's spending one night with her in her apartments in the Louvre in December 1637. There was more to this than the accident of a storm and the machinations of Guitot, the captain of his guard: Louis had become more convinced of Anne's loyalty and willingness to please him and he had begun to listen to those who stressed the danger to France if his weak-willed but unpredictable and irresponsible brother Gaston became the next ruler.

The Queen's pregnancy, highly publicized, was popular; prayers for a boy were fervent and seemed answered when Louis, a Sunday's child, was born. He was soon spoken of as 'God's gift to the nation,' and *Louis le Dieu-Donné* was the name given him at his ceremonial baptism in 1643 (the French custom being that royal children were privately christened at birth but not formally baptized till later, usually at the age of seven, 'the age of reason'). The celebrations in 1638 were many and varied; they included a Paris illumination which depicted French hopes in allegorical form – a rising sun was seen emerging from a cloud. News of the royal infant was eagerly given and eagerly received. The facts that he was strong, born with a healthy appetite and with two teeth already descended into the gums, were remarked upon, and passed on with a political twist by at least one diplomat: was this a sign that Louis as a ruler would prove rapacious, tearing the very fabric of Europe? French successes from 1637 onwards in the military field seemed to presage a growth of French

Opposite, top: The hope for a Dauphin. Allegorical figure of 'pregnant France', with dancing children. Note the violin, Queen Anne's favourite musical instrument. Below: Louis being put into his father's arms. Engraving, 1638, by Abraham Bosse. The heir presumptive to the throne was, from the early fourteenth century onwards, usually given the title Dauphin (Dolphin) of France: hence the prominent dolphin motif of the frames of both engravings.

Louis and his mother, Anne of Austria. Medal by J. Varin.

influence. Would France become the next 'exorbitant' power, that is, one that aimed at more than its fair share of European territory?

The appetite and the precocious teeth certainly gave the royal infant's wet-nurses immediate trouble. It is known that he had eight of them before he was weaned – lacerated nipples being painful enough to detract from the honour of having been chosen to feed a future king of France. The Queen, who according to prevalent custom did not breastfeed her children, loved and adored him. Her pride was gratified by the importance which now attached to her as the mother of the heir to the crown, but her delight in having someone on whom her long frustrated feelings of tenderness could focus more than matched that pride.

LOUIS' INFANCY

Anne did not take her responsibilities lightly. She was pleased when a second son, Philippe, was born in September 1640, but her sense of having to safeguard the rights of the first-born contributed to a treatment of the second boy which encouraged and possibly exaggerated a feminine streak in his nature. The hostility and jealousy of Louis XIII's own younger brother, Gaston, had been an object-lesson to all at court: he was always mixed up in intrigues, apparently over-eager to assume the reins of government. Contemporary educational theories were much concerned with the best way to bring up a future king: how could he be made fit to rule and yet preserve enough humility to prevent his turning into a tyrant? Similar speculation, if less systematic in

PHILIPPE, THE YOUNGER BROTHER

terms of results, centred round the problem of bringing up younger sons in royal families: how could these be educated so as to pose no threat to the elder when he rose to the station to which God had called him? Anne's way was to keep Philippe in petticoats beyond the usual age of discarding them (which was five), and to treat him more or less as a daughter in the hope that this might render him docile and unlikely to make trouble for Louis. Philippe's life-long interest in clothes, ribbons and decorations has been attributed to this, as has his homosexuality. Too much can be made of Anne's responsibility, as indeed of the homosexuality and feminine aspect of Philippe's nature. The emotional disposition to fall in love with young and handsome men was probably environmental in the sense that as an adolescent he found a homosexual clique at court; whether that love found physical expression is something that cannot be ascertained, though it was widely believed that it did. He had eleven children by his two wives; of these, two daughters by the English princess Henrietta, and a son and daughter by Liselotte von der Pfalz (Elisabeth-Charlotte, Princess Palatine) were alive at birth or survived infancy. That he had to brace his courage on the wedding night of his second marriage may be explained by his aesthetic aversion to this fat, plain and somewhat rustic lady when compared to the beautiful and witty Henrietta. When he and Liselotte were both old, he rather touchingly told her – though she was not moved, just horrified in her robustly Protestant and common-sense soul, as her letter recounting the story shows – that he had succeeded thanks to a sacred relic strategically placed.

If Anne can be criticized for her upbringing of Philippe, it ought perhaps to be for having failed – as so many mothers before and after her – to make him sufficiently independent of her emotionally; he certainly worshipped her to the end of her days. Again, it is easy to see how this happened: Louis had to be prepared for kingship and was given his own staff and household at seven years of age; Philippe could stay with the women as company for the Queen. He was doted on by his mother in ways which subtly differed from the love mixed with respect she showed the elder son born to be king; Philippe was gay, affectionate and a bit of a chatterbox, without Louis' shyness, *gravitas* and reserve, his good looks not spoilt, as were those of Louis, by an attack of smallpox suffered in 1647. Philippe's character was complex; he had a great love of beauty and art; he had exquisite taste and was deeply absorbed in the furnishing and decoration of his château at Saint-Cloud, but he had also a most unfeminine martial courage. This was proved in the Dutch war of 1672–78 when, in command, he insisted on taking a gamble which came off and resulted in victory at Mont Cassel. The elder brother suffered some pangs of jealousy and became aware of a gnawing uncertainty as to his own courage which could not be put to the test: as king he had been advised, a year earlier when battle with the enemy offered at Heurtebise, not to risk his life for fear of the effects on French morale if he were killed in the engagement. He accepted the advice. The fact that he had asked for guidance seems, however, to have rankled with him: he had not proved himself in battle. Whether he could have done so, given the way he had been conditioned 'to put France first', is another matter which brings us – as in the case of Philippe – to that debatable field where hereditary disposition and behavioural patterns meet and where no firm answers can be found. That Louis'

The two brothers: Louis and Philippe. Boys were customarily dressed in skirts till five years of age. Note the *fleurs de lis* on the Dauphin's cloak, the live lilies and Louis' pet dog.

jealousy should have been strong enough to deny Philippe any further opportunity to shine in military action, thus (as has been maintained) condemning him to a life of frivolity and perverting his personality, seems untenable in view of the fact that Philippe was given command in the Nine Years War over the army charged with the task of guarding the French Channel coast against invasion by the Maritime Powers. Philippe's character and interests were in any case formed early, and both brothers were to a large extent the prisoners of their roles as 'children of France' at this given time: the younger brother could not be put in a position where, as a war-hero, he might pose a threat to Louis.

The brothers usually got on well together, both in childhood and as adults. Philippe was loyal, and Louis took infinite pains to solve crises within his brother's household when sisters-in-law, wounded in their pride, complained of Philippe's favourites. He himself had few quarrels with Philippe though there were some in middle age over the behaviour of and opportunities for their respective children. The worst, and last, occurred in 1701 when Louis dared to criticize Philippe's son for neglect of his wife, who was the King's youngest legitimized daughter. This proved too much for Philippe, who tartly reminded Louis of the many marital infidelities of his own youth. Both lost their tempers and a shouting match followed. That night Philippe died of a stroke, brought on, it would seem, by the quarrel.

LOUIS' PARENTS

In his occasional emotional outbursts Philippe reminds us of his father. Louis XIII's rather inadequate feelings towards his wife had at times found outlet in strident criticism of the way she brought up the children, and especially Louis. When the boy was at the stage of being shy of adults he did not see every day, the King created a scene and complained bitterly that the Dauphin was being taught to show hostility to his father and his father's friends. Such occurrences, described in memoirs and reported (without insight) in the King's letters to Richelieu, have coloured interpretations of the relationship between Louis XIII and his son. Some historians speak of the 'hatred' between them; others, following Saint-Simon, hold that Louis XIV did not honour the memory of his father and never mentioned his name. This is not well founded. If one reads on in Louis XIII's correspondence with Richelieu, one meets a mollified father, happy in playing with a small child now accustomed to him; and, as for Louis XIV, he insisted, against the advice of his experts, on keeping his father's little château at Versailles as it had been left. The new palace had to be built round Louis XIII's creation, encircling it, to quote art historians, 'as the jewel in the centre of a diadem'. Louis' words were more direct: 'If you tear it down', he warned his architects, 'I'll have it built up again, brick by brick.'

What Louis XIV inherited of his father's genes or disposition is less easy to decide. Physically they were not alike. The father died when the boy was only four years old, and the two strong similarities – their love of hunting and their prowess at riding – can be explained by their profession: nearly all the rulers of their epoch shared a passion for one or the other since both ensured a measure of privacy and freedom of action, luxuries in the everyday life of the seventeenth-century monarch on whom government made great demands. The legend of Louis XIII's hunting exploits was much recounted, especially that of his having killed six wolves in one day; and one of Louis XIV's treasured possessions as a boy was an arquebus with which he was permitted to shoot at sparrows in the Tuileries gardens: it had been wrought and whittled in his father's workshop. Louis' delight in and aptitude for music and song can, with reasonable certainty, be attributed to the father's side of the family: Queen Anne liked music, especially that of violins, but Louis XIII was a gifted musician and composer.

Physically there were strong resemblances between Louis XIV and his mother, noticeable especially as Louis grew older, in the large appetite and the tendency to plumpness, in the long nose and the heavy jaw; and since as Queen-Regent she guided his life – and indeed in many ways controlled it – till he became an adult, she had a more discernible impact. She chose his governors and his servants and had a say in his education. Like other royal

Louis' father: Louis XIII. Detail of a portrait by Philippe de Champaigne.

mothers of the period she undertook his religious instruction in the early years and made him strongly aware of his duty to observe the rules of devotion and the teachings of the Church. Those who knew him well in his manhood thought he was without a religious temperament, but he was meticulous in attendance at services and increasingly found comfort in his task as a ruler in the thought that 'God governed all'. From as far back as he could remember, he had been told, as were most other heirs to crowns in the seventeenth century, that he owed his position not to any particular merit in himself but to God's having chosen him for the task; and it was emphasized that he would be held responsible to God for what he did as a monarch. This tenet, with a strong stress on his duty to do what was good for France rather than to follow his own inclinations, was the means of disciplining the child as he entered his teens and the need for an early majority loomed. That this lesson was learnt is shown at the first real crisis, when he was twenty-one, between Louis and those who had brought him up and educated him.

From earliest childhood Louis proved a manly boy, delighting in outdoor physical exercise. Traditional ideas of kingship and the actual war-situation centred much of his play activities on soldiering. From drumming round the garden and marching and drilling with small friends at court, he proceeded to lessons in riding and to the inspection of troops at reviews. A remarkable set of soldiers, foot and horse, with equipment and ordnance, was fashioned in silver for him – the army of France faithfully reproduced in miniature. A small fort with real cannon was later constructed for him and his playmates in the grounds of the Palais Royal, and blanks were issued for firing. When Louis, at the age of seven, was given his own household ('taken away from the women', to use the contemporary phrase), target practice began in earnest and he soon became a fine shot. As he grew older, systematic training in the chivalrous arts of horsemanship, fencing and dancing was much enjoyed. To keep himself fit and to excel in these arts, he exercised in the early morning in a room set aside as a gymnasium with vaulting horses and other apparatus, and was later in the day put through the tough school of the best riding masters. Dogs and horses were gifts which he early appreciated and liked to bestow in later years. The crisis in a childhood illness (the smallpox of 1647) was felt to have been safely passed when he weakly asked for his new English pony to be brought into his room; and he always kept up the habit of feeding his favourite dogs himself.

As a small boy Louis – like all children – enjoyed being told stories and having tales read to him. While he was with the women, fairy tales predominated, his favourite being *Peau d'Ane*, a version of the perennial theme of virtue rewarded: the beautiful, good girl, so poor that she has to wrap herself in a cloak made from the skin of an ass, is – after adventures and vicissitudes – revealed to be of royal birth and marries the hero-prince. After 1645 his valet La Porte (the servant who had once perjured himself for Queen Anne's sake) began to recount chapters of Mézeray's newly published *Histoire de France* when settling his charge for the night. These selections were edited in the sense that La Porte, who had discussed the project and Louis' character with the Queen, used the chapters to set up ideals to be followed: the worst sin was to be a king without independence, a *roi fainéant*, who let favourites decide for him. Louis' preceptor, Hardouin de Péréfixe, used a similar approach in history lessons, writing a book on the reign of Henri IV for the express purpose of presenting Louis' grandfather as a model to emulate: a fine horseman and soldier, active in war and peace, energetically pursuing the good of his people. The practice of being read to was one that Louis continued into adult life. Such reading was in part a matter of saving time; the *Gazette de Hollande*, with its wide-ranging news items, was habitually read to him in the hour before supper by his current chief adviser on foreign affairs, so that the King might ask questions or discuss problems. But that pleasure was also involved is clear from the fact that Louis frequently asked Racine and Boileau to read to him, and occasionally also Molière and Quinault.

A feeling for the French language and familiarity with classical concepts were the chief consequences of Louis' early education. Both were in part inculcated by the plays of Corneille and the explanation of his themes rather than by direct lessons; just as Louis' passionate interest in the arts was awakened by the collections he was shown and the discussions he heard among those set in control over him in childhood. Formal teaching was limited to languages (French, Italian, Spanish and Latin), mathematics, drawing and music, and some geography. It was in any case cut short in Louis' tenth year when the civil wars of the *Frondes* erupted; when these were over, his more practical education in statesmanship had to take first place, as he was already a king declared of age. Louis himself deplored the gaps in his knowledge and, to some extent, over-compensated for them in the plans he drew up for the formal education of his heirs-apparent. In some degree he also exaggerated what a prolonged formal education might have done for him. It would probably have rendered him more proficient in Latin. His Italian was good and his Spanish adequate, but his Latin remained poor. He was not mathematically inclined, nor trained at any advanced level. This counted against him in the field of military science though it did not preclude his grasping the principles of the art of war, especially of siege warfare and logistics, when these were explained to him. His inclinations were on the whole practical and sensual rather than speculative and scholarly. He learnt, in the fields where duty rather than pleasure beckoned, by application: he read reports, he listened to what he was told and then pondered and looked, gaining most from experience recollected. There is a telling phrase in one of his letters from 1680 when he had visited Dunkirk to inspect the French fleet and had gone aboard *l'Entreprenante*: 'Now all the papers about naval matters have become so much clearer to me.' He had a facility for mugging up a subject when it was necessary and dropping it again, and of finding the right men to help him.

Where Louis the ruler was personally interested, he needed no spur and took the initiative himself. He cared passionately for all the arts, and for the clarity and precision of the French language. In the dictation of his memoirs and in the discussion of chapters drafted by his historiographers, he showed keen concern for style and the meaning of words. He never was, nor thought of himself – in spite of the vast collection of books and manuscripts which were collected on his behalf – as a bookish man. But he got great satisfaction from practising

Frontispiece for Corneille's *Le Cid*. Louis' education left him with a love for and an abiding interest in the beauty and clarity of the French language. The themes of Corneille's plays – the struggle between duty and inclination, the demands of the concepts of *gloire* and of the *honnête homme* – he related to his own position and character.

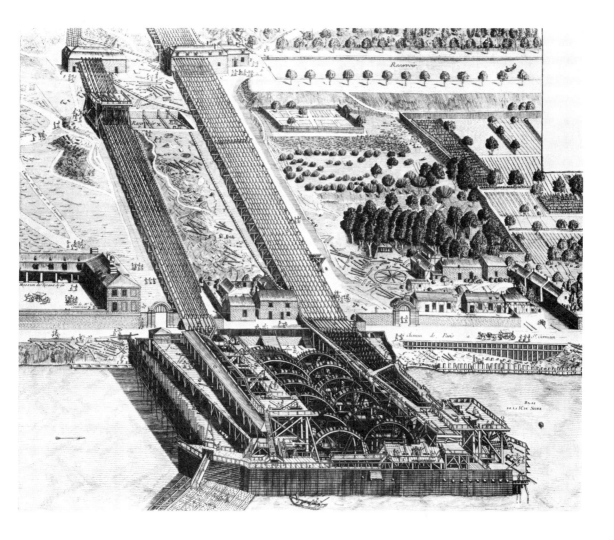

his *métier* of kingship and discovered new interests throughout his life: botany became a hobby as he discussed experiments with La Quintinie that related to his own gardens; the sciences came alive as his patronage of societies brought with it official support of the Academy of Science and as building works and other projects (such as the machine of Marly, or the canal which was dug to connect the Atlantic with the Mediterranean during his reign) caught his attention; geography began to mean more with the fine charts and maps and globes which were, in part, the result of French expeditions and conquests overseas. While Louis' very position thus widened his horizons, it also narrowed them, as we shall have reason to explore, in two interrelated, significant respects: in the realm of religious and political thought. Here Louis had to, or conceived of himself as having to, close part of his own mind to sustain the cohesion of the state entrusted to him.

Some lessons of childhood were assimilated rather than taught, picked up

The so-called *Machine de Marly*, completed in 1682, which brought water from the Seine to Versailles.

The father-figure: Cardinal Mazarin with Louis. Engraving (anonymous) to commemorate Mazarin's taking charge of the Dauphin's education.

from attendants and from Queen Anne and her chief adviser, Cardinal Mazarin. Louis early learnt to guard his tongue and to suppress information. This was in part drilled into him by those who served him, since they found it wearisome to guard their own tongues rigorously in the presence of the child: they and Louis had got into hot water when the boy let slip, in his mother's presence, the nickname 'the Grand Turk' by which Mazarin was known among those who distrusted or disliked the former papal diplomat, powerful even before Richelieu's death and even more so after Louis XIII's. Richelieu had, on his death-bed in December 1642, begged Louis XIII to trust Mazarin's advice and expertise concerning affairs both at home and abroad, and the King significantly named Mazarin godfather to his son in that formal baptism which took place on 21 April 1643, once Louis XIII felt sure he himself would not survive till the Dauphin reached the age of seven. He also included Mazarin among the regents named for the minority, which began on 14 May of that year.

It used to be believed (and is still held by some historians of the period) that Mazarin also became Louis XIV's stepfather by a secret marriage to Queen Anne. Recently, however, such weighty arguments have been marshalled against this hypothesis that it seems no longer tenable. Mazarin, though not a priest, was determined to remain unmarried lest he lack the qualification of celibacy if ever the chance came, as he hoped, to stand for election as Pope. The intense pride of Anne in her own royal blood created another obstacle to marriage and even to a physical relationship between herself and the relatively humbly born Italian who had made his way in the world thanks to his outstanding ability. Her own growing piety and self-control after Louis XIII's death would point in the same direction. Anne, like Mazarin, was not above dissimulation – indeed this was one lesson both of them, involuntarily, taught Louis XIV – but her answer to a close woman friend, who taxed her with love for Mazarin, has the ring of truth, 'I admit that I like him and feel tender towards him, but my affection does not amount to love, or if it does it is without my knowledge. My senses are not involved, though my mind is charmed by his mind.'

Mazarin's was a well-stocked mind. He was widely read, a collector of books and manuscripts, a lover of music, opera and theatre. He had the finest of clothes, the choicest of scents, the best of tastes. His gentleness as well as his *esprit* appealed to the Queen. It also counted that they could speak Spanish together and that his first diplomatic mission had been to her never forgotten homeland. Though not a naturalized Frenchman, he owed a gratitude to France and to her late husband. It was French efforts which had obtained the coveted cardinal's hat for him, and it was opportunities ruthlessly exploited in France which had enabled him to amass the fortune that let him indulge in his chief pleasures: the building and furnishing of palaces and the collecting of works of art and precious stones, especially diamonds of the highest quality. His friendship and support, his political and administrative experience, his guile, riches, contacts and clients became indispensable for the shrewd but untrained Queen determined to safeguard her son's heritage. Personal and political considerations here gave them a joint objective. Together they set aside the regency council nominated in Louis XIII's will* and Anne became sole regent until Louis should be declared of age.

For Louis, Mazarin became the teacher of statecraft, the man who trained him for his position as king. This took place on three levels. The unconscious example lay in Mazarin's behaviour: kind and gracious, he seemed to give way but was in reality pursuing firm goals persistently; his ability to impress and influence by the excellence of his taste and the size of his fortune also counted. Directly and practically Mazarin gradually introduced Louis to affairs of state, to the value of ceremonial, to the conduct of council meetings, to the analyses of dispatches received and to the ways in which instructions should be drafted; by the time Louis was sixteen he spent at least two hours a day (from 9 to 11 in the morning) with Mazarin learning how policy decisions were made. Finally Louis experienced at Mazarin's hands (mainly by skilfully phrased letters) the breaking of his own will. He confessed in the instructions penned for his own son that he had hated the Cardinal for this at the time, but had lived to bless him for the lesson that France came before the king's personal inclinations.

That Louis never totally identified with Mazarin even as a child was due to his own less intellectually motivated temperament. Mazarin, with his ingratiating mild manner, did not measure up to soldier-heroes like Henri IV, and Louis grew up in years when – though peace negotiations got under way in Germany from 1643–44 onwards – the talk at court was of bravery in action, and of the *gloire* of French arms. In retrospect Louis also blamed Mazarin for having profited too selfishly from his position, leaving the crown impoverished and the state indebted.

Civil war, the most horrible of all forms of war, was experienced by the royal family in a more direct way than the war against the foreign enemies. Indeed the first *Fronde*† erupted just as France seemed to have got the measure of its enemies abroad; at Rocroi, in the Spanish Netherlands, a French army had decisively beaten Philip IV's forces in 1643; in Germany the French and the Swedes had the upper hand and used military diversions mainly as a means to prod the peace negotiations along. Unrest at home was caused in the first place by the taxes made necessary by the war abroad. These hit, directly or indirectly, both well-to-do and poor; the non-privileged carried the heavier burden of direct taxation, but the clergy could be asked for more generous gifts to the state in war-time and noblemen could be moved in various ways to help finance the war effort. Office-holders could be, and were, milked, whenever the *paulette* (an annual tribute paid to ensure that bought offices could be passed on to heirs) came up for periodic renewal, as it did in 1648. The actual increase decreed in May of that year on a certain body of office-holders, those of the

CIVIL WAR.
THE FRONDES 1648-52

* Anne and Mazarin were both named, as were three Richelieu-trained administrators, but so were two of the princes of the blood, Louis XIII's brother Gaston and his cousin Henri II de Bourbon, prince de Condé. Queen and Cardinal alike feared that Gaston and Condé would topple Mazarin and put a stop to the centralizing processes of Louis XIII's reign.

† The word *Fronde* (catapult, sling) was – as in the case of Whigs and Tories – originally pejorative, but *frondeurs* soon began to sport sashes embroidered with slings.

Louis XIV and the Queen-Regent receiving homage from the duc de Beaufort, Paul Gondi, the Coadjutor Archbishop of Paris (later Cardinal de Retz), and Mr de la Motte. Note in the royal party Louis' brother Philippe, his uncle Gaston d'Orléans and his governor Villeroi.

Below: Louis XIV as a minor. Representative portrait by Mignard; note the fine clothes, the jewelled brooches and the symbols of majesty; also the facial similarity with the crude print above.

Below right: Louis XIV as victor over the Fronde. Later allegorical painting.

Within the image banner: REIOVISSANCE GENERALLE DES FRANCOIS TOVCHANT LA PAIX

General rejoicing at the Peace of 1648.

sovereign courts, was slight but sufficient to provoke the Paris Parlement into establishing a committee to reform the government of France. By June its delegates had drawn up a charter which aimed at undoing the work of the Bourbon dynasty: the system of royal inspectors, the *intendants*, sent on missions to the provinces by Richelieu must come to an end, control over taxation must revert to the Estates (not called since 1614) or be handed over to the Parlement. Dissatisfaction focused on Mazarin, the foreigner, who was making himself rich while France groaned under the war-time burden. Unrest spread to other Parlements and to the poorer classes in Paris and elsewhere (in Bordeaux and Marseilles, for instance, there were serious semi-republican and radical risings during the *Frondes*). More significantly, it also unsettled the high nobility, who felt that Mazarin had usurped the right of the princes of the blood to advise Queen Anne. Why was he bringing members of his own family to Paris: was he trying to found a dynasty of favourites? Such questions were important for a class which held life to be unbearable if honour were slighted, and gave an added spur to the traditional attempts of the high nobility to carve out autonomous states or provinces inside France in times of royal minorities.

Anne, taking Mazarin's advice, gave way over the *intendants*, but as Parlement still insisted on a constitutional charter to circumscribe the power of the crown, she – against Mazarin's advice but heartened by Condé's victory at Lens over the Spaniards – ordered the arrest of three of its leaders, among them the revered Broussel and Paul de Gondi, Coadjutor Archbishop of Paris (the later Cardinal de Retz). These arrests resulted in barricades and riot. The prisoners were released, but civil war broke out. It was to last for four long years, the *Fronde parlementaire* of 1648–49 merging into the *Fronde* of the princes, 1650–52.

The effects of the *Frondes* on Louis XIV have been much debated, and though the civil wars will not here be narrated in any detail, reference must be made to certain incidents during the series of wars fought out between the royal family and its adherents on the one hand and changing coalitions of *frondeurs* on the other. Only then can the effect on Louis be put into perspective.

21

In one sense, Louis' childhood came to an end with the outbreak of the *Frondes*. It was not only that life became insecure and unpleasant – a fate meted out to many children in all ages – but that Louis had to be taken into the confidence of his mother and Mazarin about political and military matters of which he could have no deep understanding.

After her husband's death Anne had moved her two sons to a smaller and gayer palace than the Louvre, the Palais Cardinal, willed by Richelieu to Louis XIII, and renamed the Palais Royal. It had pleasant grounds and its own theatre. Here Louis and Philippe played in the gardens and had their first taste of ballets and plays. In the civil war Anne and her two sons, but especially Louis, became prizes for whom warring factions fought. The family home became at times a near-prison when Paris had to be abandoned, not in carefree outings to other châteaux but in humiliating flights: for a short period in September 1648, for half a year from January 1649, for three months after July 1652. Heroes of the war against the foreign enemies changed sides. For love of a lady *frondeur* (Condé's sister, Anne-Geneviève de Bourbon-Condé, duchesse de Longueville), the vicomte de Turenne hurried from Germany with an army of mercenaries to help the cause she had espoused, and though Mazarin's money dispersed the soldiers, Turenne became a *frondeur*. The great Condé himself, like all the princes of the blood, despised Mazarin, but stayed loyal to the crown because his brother Conti (with whom he was in dispute over their father's will) was a *Fronde* leader; he therefore helped to bring the *Fronde parlementaire* to an end by a show of force.

Between August 1649 and January 1650, however, Condé's determination to topple Mazarin became clear enough for Anne to decide that he would have to be stopped before he became dangerous to the crown itself: he was the fourth in the line of succession and was already asking favours and positions which threatened to interfere with the powers of the king. Louis was not asked – as some biographies state – to dissimulate friendship with Condé at the council meeting at which he, Conti and Longueville were arrested. Louis and Anne were in fact at prayer till the arrests had been made, but the reasons for the action had been explained to Louis and shortly afterwards he accompanied his mother and the royal army on a campaign to Normandy and Burgundy to intimidate or subdue the military forces of the Condé family and other noble *frondeurs* in these provinces. Here Louis first heard shots fired in anger and witnessed their effect: during an inspection of the royal troops besieging Bellegarde, an officer standing close by him was killed by fire from the walls of the fortress.

In February 1651 dissimulation had to be taught. Paris was once more in the grip of anti-Mazarin sentiment. The Parlement petitioned the Queen to dismiss Mazarin and release Condé and his fellow-prisoners. Mazarin fled and – in fear of becoming a prisoner herself – Anne decided in the night of 9–10 February to take her children out of the capital and meet Mazarin at a prearranged place in the country. Louis was already booted and dressed when, alerted by rumours of the impending flight, crowds surrounded the Palais Royal, hammered on its doors and shouted demands to see the King. His uncle Gaston had already been prevailed upon to close the gates of Paris and

Le Grand Condé: Louis II de Bourbon, prince de Condé on his father's death in 1646. He was honoured for his victories at Rocroi (1643) and at Lens (1648), feared for his ambition, disliked for his pride and likened – because of his prominent nose and receding chin – to a bird of prey. His desertion to the Spanish side was condoned at the Peace of the Pyrenees (1659). Bust by Coysevox.

to send a captain of his guards to investigate the rumours. The Queen-Regent kept her nerve, had Louis covered up in bed and ordered him to pretend to be asleep. The officer was permitted to see Louis, by the light of a candle and with a corner of the bed-curtains lifted, apparently in sound sleep. The crowd proved unwilling to rely on the captain's word; a delegation was then allowed to file past the royal bed and make sure that the King was within.

The royal family being virtually imprisoned in Paris, Mazarin attempted reconciliation with Condé at the cost of freeing him, his brother and his brother-in-law. Condé, offended, refused to discuss terms and rode straight to Paris to take charge of the *Fronde* of the princes. Mazarin went into exile, to the territories of the Archbishop-Elector of Cologne, whence he corresponded with the Queen. Both bided their time till Louis could be declared of age; this was done at the earliest possible moment, on 7 September 1651 when the boy had just entered his fourteenth year, the solemn declaration being followed by tournaments, ballets and other temporal celebrations. Louis danced his first ballet in public and was permitted to play cards for money.

LOUIS DECLARED OF AGE

With Louis a major in law, Mazarin felt strong enough to hire a private army to invade France to 'free the King'. His action had the effect of bringing Gaston and his formidable daughter, Anne-Marie-Louise (*Mademoiselle* in court parlance), more openly into Condé's camp. Turenne, however, came back to the side of the court, his soldier's loyalty preventing him fighting the person of a king who, in the contemporary phrase, 'had entered into his own'. Turenne, indeed, saved the royal cause, though Paris was lost (temporarily) to Condé on 2 July 1652. The battle for the capital took place just outside the gate of Saint-Antoine, with the King and Mazarin, and other members of the court, watching from the hill of Charonne. The fight seemed to be going in favour of the royal army, which was superior in numbers and well-trained, but suddenly the cannon of the eight-towered Bastille fortress began to fire on Turenne's men, causing dreadful casualties. The treachery had come from within the royal family: Mademoiselle had obtained written full powers from Gaston which enabled her to gain entrance to the Bastille and order the training and firing of the cannon as she thought fit. In the resulting confusion the gate of Saint-Antoine was opened to permit Condé's army to enter Paris in triumph, preventing the return of the King and his party.

Turenne's firmness and leadership proved invaluable in the months that followed. Mazarin, momentarily shattered by the death of his nephew Paul Mancini – a victim of the Bastille cannon – in the battle of Saint-Antoine, realized, when recovering, that he must keep in the background to permit a settlement between the court and the *frondeurs*. Turenne was aided by the conflicting interests of the Paris Parlement and the high nobility and by the increasing awareness, in Paris as elsewhere in France, that the *frondeurs*, whether of the *noblesse de l'épée*, of the *noblesse de la robe*, or of the radicals, were playing into the hands of the king of Spain. Charles, duke of Lorraine, was financed by Philip IV and commissioned to join Condé's army outside Paris for the purpose of extending *frondeur* control over wider areas of France, and – if possible – to link up with other centres of anti-royalist opposition, such as Bordeaux and Marseilles. Meanwhile Philip IV's own troops reconquered Dunkirk and Gravelines in the Southern Netherlands. Turenne was not strong enough to fight the combined forces of Lorraine and Condé, but managed to prevent their junction and give time for negotiations between the court and the Parlement to mature.

On 21 October Louis XIV returned to Paris. The next day a general amnesty, with a few named exceptions, was proclaimed in a *lit de justice* and terms laid down which, for the future, limited the role of the Parlement to that of registering royal acts. In 1641 Richelieu had deprived the Parlement of its right to discuss policy matters. This ban was now reinforced and, moreover, its members were specifically forbidden to meddle in matters of finance. While the Parlement willingly accepted a royal prohibition of commerce between itself and the princes of the blood, there was strong resentment at the refusal to meet its constitutionalist demands. Fear of renewed unrest made the court break, if not its given word, at least its implied pardon for Cardinal de Retz. His name had not been on the list of those excluded from the amnesty; nevertheless he was arrested and imprisoned. Even with Retz out of play, attempts were made

to regain for Parlement the right to discuss financial matters and thus influence policy: it was only just, it was argued, that Parlement should 'examine' finance bills laid before it for registration.

In 1655 this issue came to a head when the *Chambre des Enquêtes* called a joint session of all chambers in the Palais de Justice without the King's approval or prior knowledge. By this time Louis XIV's authority had been further strengthened by his consecration as king in Rheims Cathedral on 7 June 1654, and the crisis was overcome by a show of royal authority diluted by tact. The King, informed at Vincennes (where he was spending the day hunting with Mazarin), galloped to Paris in hunting costume, strode into the assembly and spoke briefly and firmly;* Turenne patiently explained the need for new taxes to pursue the war against Spain; Mazarin judiciously dispensed presents and warned of the dangers of a new *Fronde*. The Paris Parlement gave in and accepted, at least for the time being, that deliberative meetings, however disguised, would not be tolerated.

The general amnesty. Contemporary print depicting the lit de justice *in the Louvre on 22 October 1652. Note the young king wearing the order of Saint-Esprit with elaborate collar.*

LOUIS ANOINTED KING

---

* Louis' speech did not contain the famous but apocryphal phrase, *L'Etat, c'est moi.* What he said was: 'Everyone knows how much trouble your meetings have caused my state and the dangerous results they have produced. I now learn that you intend to continue such meetings on the pretext of discussing edicts which were proclaimed and read here in my presence only a short while ago. I have come today expressly to forbid you to do this. I absolutely forbid it and I forbid you, Monsieur le Premier President, to permit or tolerate it, whatever pressure *Messieurs des Enquêtes* exert on you.'

To vanquish Spain, not broken by the Portuguese and Catalonian revolts which France had supported from 1640 onwards, Mazarin entered into an alliance with Cromwell's England, thus gaining for France the support of a strong naval power. The price for this alliance was an agreement that Dunkirk, when taken from Spain, should become English. This was indeed secured by the Peace of the Pyrenees in 1659, when Jamaica was added in recognition of English victories in the West Indies. At that peace France had Cerdagne and Roussillon returned to her, while parts of Artois, Flanders, Hainault and Luxembourg were gained against a pardon (which implied restoration to estates and positions) for those *frondeurs* who had fought with Spain, Condé being particularly named. Charles, duke of Lorraine, Philip IV's ally, had to give up a considerable part of his duchy to France. 'Military roads' to permit passage of troops to Metz and Alsace were also ceded and France's right to occupy the whole duchy, if its ruler cooperated with the enemies of France, was recorded.

Gratitude to and respect for Turenne was one obvious outcome of the *Frondes* for Louis. Another was the young King's decision to move back to the Louvre. The Palais Royal, he complained, was a private house, without even a moat for defence. The memory of having seen Frenchmen fighting Frenchmen stayed with him. Unity and consensus became a near-obsession with him in later years and influenced his policy towards Jansenists and Huguenots in particular. In his heart he never trusted any of those who had carried arms against France with the Spaniards and he was especially wary of Condé. He feared the divisive aims – if seen from his own position – of the high nobility and became resolved, when the chance offered, to rule on his own so that there should be no further excuse for *Frondes*: if there were no first minister who could be blamed for taking the king's confidence away from his subjects, high and low, the power of the crown could more easily be maintained. The *Frondes* thus reinforced those lessons implanted which were acceptable to his temperament: reliance on good sense, on reason and the 'right balance', and concern for the *métier* of the king, the professional exercise of his public duty for which God would grant him the necessary wisdom.

For Queen Anne the *Frondes* had brought renewed emotional conflict. Her brother Philip IV had supported the French high noble rebels and made use of them. Her wish was now for a Franco-Spanish reconciliation; her dream that Louis should marry the elder of Philip's daughters, exactly his own age, to mark that reconciliation. She painted for her son the glories, the treasures, the proud traditions of Spain in such a way that when the time came for him to choose between the dictates of his own heart and so prestigious a family dynastic alliance, duty – after a hard fight – won. Mazarin also stressed the future benefits of a Spanish marriage: if the male descendants of Philip IV died out, the claim of Louis, and of his children, to the Spanish succession, or to part of it, would be strengthened and France might at last be free of one Habsburg neighbour.

Louis himself had seen something of the possible 'Spanish inheritance' when in 1657 he had been present at the siege of Montmédy in Luxembourg. He saw more in the summer of 1658 when he joined the French army in the

Opposite: Consecration of Louis XIV in Rheims Cathedral, 7 June 1654. As an anointed king, Louis two days later for the first time touched for scrofula with the old phrase *Le roi te touche, Dieu te guérit*. The number of sufferers had accumulated during the years of the minority and 3,000 presented themselves on this occasion. Throughout Louis' reign, sick people came to his court to be touched, also from Spain and the German states. The last time Louis performed the ceremony (for 1,700) was 8 June 1715.

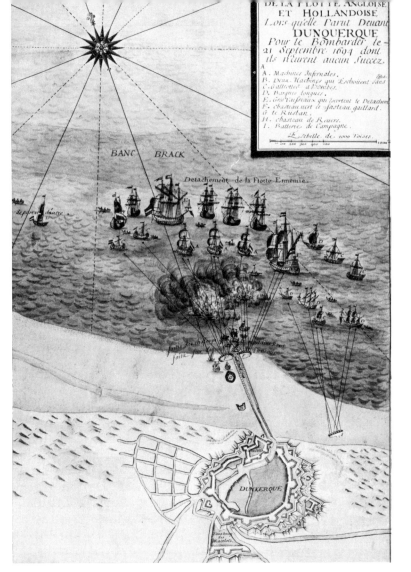

DE LA FLOTTE ANGLOISE
ET HOLLANDOISE
Lors qu'elle Parut Devant
DUNQUERQUE
Pour le Bombarder le
21 Septembre 1694 dont
ils n'eurent aucun Succez.

A.
A. Machines Infernales.
B. Deux Machines qui Eschouent sans
C. Galliotes à Bombes.
D. Barques longues.
E. Gros vaisseaux qui favorisent le Detachement
F. chasteau vert le chasteau gaillard.
à le Risban.
H. chasteau de Rouere.
I. Batteries de Campagne.
L'echelle de 1000 Toises.

BANC BRACK

Detachement de la Flotte Ennemie.

DUNKERQUE

Dunkirk. Here depicted in 1694 when a combined Anglo-Dutch fleet bombarded the port. William III much regretted Charles II's sale, since in Louis' hands Dunkirk became a safe refuge for French privateers in wartime. During the negotiations for the partition treaties (see text, p. 86) William hinted (though without much hope of success) that he would make big concessions to Louis if, in exchange, 'I could have Dunkirk.'

Southern Netherlands at the siege of Dunkirk and the nearby Mardyck, blockaded from the sea by Cromwell's navy. His presence at this campaign proved a stepping-stone towards independence from both mother and teacher: here was a field where Mazarin, who accompanied him, was no expert and where queens had no place. It was not Louis' first sight of the sea. There had been a brief boyhood visit to Dieppe in 1647 with the Queen-Regent when he received the present of a Swedish naval ship and took part in a mock sea battle. Now, at the age of twenty, he looked at the sea with grown-up eyes, became entranced with the aesthetic beauty of a fleet under full sail and aware of navies as instruments of policy. His later decision to offer Charles II of England a large sum of money for Dunkirk was a personal one and the role of French Dunkirk after 1662 was significant in peace and war.

Those in charge of Louis' safety in 1658 were afraid of exposing him to danger and he was not active in the battle of the Dunes (14 June) when

Turenne brilliantly defeated the Spanish attempt, in which Condé took part, to raise the French siege. He was, however, allowed to visit the trenches and began a life-long interest in sieges. Neither bullet nor ball laid him low, but a fever (probably typhoid), picked up at Mardyck, brought him to death's door. His recovery was slow; he looks pale and unfit, pasty-faced and ill at ease in a sketch which Le Brun made of him during the convalescence at Compiègne, renowned for its 'good air'.

In retrospect Louis drew other lessons from the *Fronde* period. The first concerned the Stuarts. One result of Mazarin's alliance with Cromwell was that Louis' male Stuart relations, in exile in France after the arrest of Charles I in 1647, left for the Spanish Netherlands and fought for Spain. In the post-Restoration years Louis XIV concluded that the fickleness of the Stuarts towards France was caused by the French desertion of their cause in the 1650s. After 1688 he determined not to repeat Mazarin's mistake: the Stuarts would not be driven out of France, however much William III pressed for their removal from French soil. The second lesson concerned money. The humiliating experience of a royal family poor in the midst of riches burnt into him as he looked back on the wealth of Mazarin, the riches of the high nobility, and of servants of the crown, such as Fouquet. He had not been bothered by his poor, patched garments which seemed most unroyal to observers in the late 1640s; what he did mind dreadfully in the late 1650s was the royal family's lack of ready cash or credit. The presents of jewellery for his Spanish bride in 1660 were, to give but one example, on a scale he regarded as incommensurate with the dignity of France. Such thoughts did not make Louis XIV a miser, but they did make him a hoarder and collector of jewellery and precious stones. Only one of his famous diamonds, the triangular *Diamant Hortensia* of 20½ carats, is still French state property, on show in the Louvre; but we know that he possessed other famous gems, including the Hope Diamond, the *Miroir du Portugal*, and the fabulous pear-shaped *Grand Sancy* of some 50 carats which had belonged to Charles the Bold; we also know that he spent 2,259,000 *livres* on precious stones alone in the short period 1665 to 1668. He became a stickler for the return of those pieces from the royal treasury which were alienated for the lifetime of this or that royal personage, or, in the case of his mistresses, for the duration of the period of their being *maîtresse en titre*. The only quarrel we know of with his brother Philippe (until those clashes over the future of their grown-up children mentioned above) took place when their mother was found to have willed all her jewellery, personal as well as that which formed part of the royal collection, to Philippe's elder daughter by his marriage to Henrietta. Philippe, who adored jewels for their own sake, was forced to give way by royal command, and only Anne's personal jewellery was handed over to Marie-Louise. Similarly, Louis' decision to have the furniture and accoutrements for his *Grande Galerie* fashioned in solid silver can be interpreted as a hedge, if not against inflation then against bad times for the monarchy or the state. It was indeed melted down when Louis needed cash during the Nine Years War to keep the French armies in the field, though modern specialists have commented on the fact that it brought in only 3 million *livres*, whereas it had cost four times that amount to fashion.

'Pearls and tears'. When Louis, in 1658, wished to give a present to Marie Mancini, he suffered from lack of money. His aunt, the Dowager-Queen Henrietta of England, exiled in France and hard up, was willing to sell her famous set of large matched pearls and Louis was forced to borrow the purchase price from Mazarin. Marie accepted the gift but, weeping, reproached Louis for letting her go. (Cf. below, p. 45.) A similar set of the period, worn by a niece of Mazarin's, Anne Martinot, princesse de Conti, is shown below.

29

Plan
Pour l'hostel
Royal des
Invalides.

In these lessons, taught or drawn for himself, lies the importance of the *Fronde* years. The one effect usually stressed – Louis' hatred of Paris and consequent determination to move out of the ancient capital as soon as possible, never to return – seems untenable. Louis, his court and his administration, were based in Paris till 1682, first in the Louvre, and then (after a fire made that palace uninhabitable in 1671) the Tuileries. The royal family spent increasingly more time at Versailles after 1674 when the Grands Appartements were ready – and in 1678 the decision to move there permanently was taken. But Louis remained profoundly interested in the development of Paris all his life: he gave Paris the Pont Royal, restored Notre Dame, completed and embellished the Louvre, laid out the Champs-Elysées in former marshland and created boulevards where he razed the old fortifications, built the Observatory and the College of the Four Nations, the Salpêtrière for the homeless and the Invalides for old soldiers. The capital also received two new gates (the Saint-Denis and the Saint-Martin), many new fountains and 5,000 street lamps lit by whale oil. Two of Paris' finest squares were laid out in his reign: the Place des Victoires in Louis' honour after the nation in 1680 had accorded the King the title of *Le Grand*; the Place Vendôme on Louis' initiative (to house the royal library, archives and various academies) but with a statue donated by the city of Paris. Even after 1682 Louis visited Paris, for religious and civic ceremonies in particular, until late middle age; from then on he preferred to send sons and grandsons to represent him and asked deputations to visit him wherever he might be.

Medal by Varin (1665) to celebrate Louis' decision to rebuild the Louvre, showing Bernini's Italianate design. This was not used, as it did not appeal to the King and his advisers.

Opposite: Print celebrating the founding of the Invalides in 1672.

Below: Gouache (anon.) showing the Seine firewood quay. Note Notre Dame, the restoration of which was completed by 1714.

View of Paris from the older, brick-built Pont Neuf. Note the Pont Royal, the first arched stone bridge over the Seine linking the left bank to the Louvre with its new, classical façade.

Below: Pompe de la Samaritaine: one of the new fountains to provide good drinking water.

The *Collège des Quatres Nations*: Close-up of the Collège (seen also in the Paris view above), financed by Mazarin's will for the education of noble youth from the four provinces which had become French by the peacemakings of 1648 and 1659. Louis in his will asked his successor to continue to benefit the Collège. It now houses the Académie Française. Engraving by Pérelle.

In 1694 Louis XIV bought the Hôtel Vendôme, and Hardouin-Mansart began to lay out the square (originally known as that of Louis le Grand). In 1699 the equestrian statue by Girardon was put in place, an occasion celebrated with illuminations, fireworks and competitions between the mariners of the Seine. The statue was destroyed during the Revolution.

View of Versailles. Note the traffic and the staircase of the hundred steps.

Opposite, above: Part of the grounds as they are today; note the raised position of the Latona group in the fountain to the right and compare it with that seen on pp. 36–37 (22). The change was made in 1680. Below: Part of Louis' guide to the grounds in his own hand.

Overleaf: Versailles, château, grounds and part of town. Note Colonnade to the right (30) and Clagny (12) built for Madame de Montespan.

Louis' decision in 1669 to rebuild his father's hunting lodge at Versailles had various motives. The little château was already dear and familiar, and the gardens – the green outdoor 'appartements' – were greatly extended and improved from 1661 onwards by Le Nôtre and used for fêtes and plays. Its fountains finally numbered more than a thousand, innumerable trees were transplanted, lakes and canals were dug and the intricate machine de Marly constructed to supply enough water. One reason for the King's decision to build was a desire to commemorate the Bourbon dynasty which – in contrast to the earlier Capetian branches – had no grand palace to its credit. It was impossible to achieve a worthy setting within Paris where private property rights even barred the way for a desirable extension to link the Louvre grounds with those of the Tuileries. Paris was, in any case, becoming increasingly inconvenient for a growing royal bureaucracy. The capital's population had grown to 450,000; congested traffic caused delays, and problems arose in respect of water-supply and sewage. It was tempting and sensible to make a new start.

Personal motives also played their part: the inclination to begin afresh, giving expression to his own taste in building as in landscape gardening and statuary; the desire to create a beautiful setting for court fêtes, celebrating (though not officially) first his love for Louise de La Vallière and then for Athénaïs de Montespan; his preference for a country life in which he could spend the always decreasing time that could be spared from work in riding, shooting, hunting with falcons and hounds, driving his wagonette skilfully and fast, or just walking in his gardens. He was proud enough of the park at Versailles to write in his own hand a Guide to Sightseers; he liked to improve on fountains

34

2. le tour et l'on sera a la colonade
en y entrant on verra le groupe
du milieu et l'on fera en suitte le
tour pour considerer les collonnes
les cintres les bas reliefs les vases
et les bassins en sortant on ira
dans l'allée royalle on s'avancera
jusques a pollon d'ou l'on verra
le costé du canal et celuy du chateau

3. on remontera apres ~~la piece de~~
on en fera le tour

4. de la on ira aux ~~bains d'apollon~~ on les
considerera aussi que la fontaine
et les bas autres coaprès en ayant
fait le tour l'on ira a flore

5. on desendra dans la salle du
conseil

1. en sortant du chateau par le vestibule
~~....~~ sous la chambre du
roy on ira sur la terrasse on
s'arretera sur le haut des degres
pour considerer les parterres
les pieces d'eau et les fontaines
des cabinets

2. apres on tournera a gauche et
l'on descendra par le degré des...
on marchera sur le haut on fera
une pose pour voir le parterre du
midy et apres on ira sur le haut
de l'orangerie d'ou l'on verra
le parterre des orangers et le lac
des suisses

3. on tournera pour aller monter a droit
sur la terrasse et l'on ira au corps
avancé d'ou l'on voit les...

and the placing of statuary; he had a passion for rare flowers, and employed La Quintinie to improve his fruit trees and took a great interest in the famous botanist's pruning technique: Dangeau, in diaries which amount to a journal of Louis XIV's activities, notes the days when the King 'went to prune his trees'. Louis in middle age has been labelled, not without some justification, *le roi propriétaire*, the king as squire, proud of his house and land and of the entertainments he could offer to court and visitors.

LOUIS IN LOVE

The emotional crisis of Louis' young manhood came at a time when the end of the war with Spain was clearly in sight. Peace negotiations had long been afoot and in 1658 they got under way properly between the representative of Philip IV, Luis de Haro, and the skilful French diplomat Hugh de Lionne. Cromwell's England was naturally represented, and though Charles Stuart – at a late stage – went in person to plead his cause he had no success with either Spain or France. Once Louis had been persuaded that a pardon for the French *frondeurs* who had served with Philip IV would be both wise and chivalrous, interest concentrated round French efforts to obtain Philip's elder daughter, Maria Teresa, as Louis' bride. Though these were eventually successful, it was no easy matter. For one thing, Maria Teresa was more or less promised to Leopold, head of the Austrian Habsburg state since 1657 and Emperor of Germany since 1658. Her sister, Margarita Teresa, would not do; she was twelve years younger than Maria Teresa, a child who could not be expected to provide France with an heir as soon as desired. To put some pressure on the Spanish court, and to provide for an alternative bride, Mazarin persuaded Queen Anne – who in her turn persuaded Louis – that the French court should travel to Lyons in the autumn of 1658 to meet the widowed duchess of Savoy (a daughter of Henri IV and thus Louis' aunt), her son, Duke Carlo Emanuele, and her two daughters, the younger of whom, Marguerite, was unmarried, for the express purpose of seeing whether she and Louis 'were suited'.

That Louis was ready for marriage was agreed by both Mazarin and Anne. Before any match could be arranged, however, Louis fell in love and asked permission to marry Mazarin's own niece, Marie Mancini. Anne was horrified: a misalliance was in any case unacceptable and even rumours of Louis' contemplating such a union might wreck the Spanish marriage project. Mazarin was against the match for political reasons, and in his letters to the Queen and Louis he stressed his niece's unsuitability by both birth and temperament to become a king's wife.

Louis' romantic, physically undemanding, love for Marie Mancini may at first sight seem strange in a young man who had lost his virginity at the age of sixteen. At that time, when he was preparing to join the army for the 1655 campaign in the Spanish Netherlands, he seems – possibly for reasons of hygiene in an age when syphilis was rampant – to have been encouraged to gain his first sexual experience with the Queen's lady of the bedchamber, Mme de Beauvais, a widow at least twenty years his senior.* Whether from her, or (as is more likely) from a partner subsequently chosen by himself, Louis picked up gonorrhea. His physician Vallot, when consulted about the King's symptoms, thought it impolite to give a straightforward explanation and suggested (ac-

Le Brun's sketch of Louis XIV during his convalescence after the 1658 fever. Note the prominent nose. There is little here of the dashing air that entranced Marie. The medals, busts and paintings of the early 1660s convey his charm better (cf. p. 43).

Three of the Mancini sisters. Though crudely painted, the liveliness of Marie (right) comes across. The bow and arrow, attributes of the hunting goddess Diana, hint at the sporting interests she shared with Louis. The sisters, Laura, Olympe, Marie, Hortense and Marie-Anne were known as the 'Mazarinettes', while the eighteen pieces of jewellery (not particularly valuable) which Mazarin left Louis from his enormous collection of choice diamonds, pearls and precious stones, were labelled 'the Mazarines'.

cording to the royal medical journal) that the trouble might be inherited or have arisen from excessive equestrian exercise. Louis soon guessed the truth, not difficult since the physician warned him that the complaint might have dire consequences for the heirs of the King's own body. It is probable, though this must remain a hypothesis which cannot be verified, that Louis' disgust and embarrassment (of which we possess evidence) at having caught venereal disease and the treatment it involved made him concentrate for some time on the non-sexual aspects of his relationship to women.

He had long enjoyed the company of the young Mazarin nieces and had been somewhat enamoured, the court believed, of the second, Olympe. Mazarin, alarmed, had married her off to the comte de Soissons: there was never any difficulty in finding princes of the blood as husbands for girls who would inherit part of Mazarin's fortune, estimated at fifty million *livres*. From 1657 Louis, by chance, began to see much of her younger sister, Marie, then seventeen years old. She was lively and opinionated, a well-read bluestocking of the *précieuse* kind. She had wept at his bedside in Calais when the fever seemed likely to kill him; she had cheered his convalescence at Compiègne and Fontainebleau; and was one of the party of young people that in October 1658 accompanied the royal progress south to meet the Savoyard relatives.

This was the longest tour the French court had undertaken in Louis' lifetime. Royal progresses were in France, as elsewhere in Europe, age-old, meant to display a new king to his country and to make the ruler acquainted with local personages and conditions. The *Frondes* and the war had hitherto limited Louis' travels to the north and they had taken the form of campaigns against either the domestic or the foreign enemy. With the end of the war with Spain

* The direct evidence for Anne's encouraging the affair is slight but the fact that she continued to hold Mme de Beauvais in high regard after the affair was common knowledge lends it support: it was from the balcony of her Paris house that Queen Anne and Mazarin watched Louis XIV's and Maria Teresa's wedding procession.

39

in sight, the journey to Lyons could be planned as a progress of peace-time character. It was an occasion for ceremonial entries, for portals and poems of welcome, for garlands of flowers and dances and other festivities in the towns and villages along the way. The assumption, often encountered, that Louis XIV throughout his reign sat like a spider at the centre of a web and never learnt anything at first hand about the twenty million Frenchmen he governed, nor of the great local variations of his kingdom, is mistaken. Indeed, if we look at a contemporary map of France hardly a province can be seen which Louis did not at one time or other visit, and many he got to know well.

Map showing the vulnerability of the northern and eastern French frontier. The 'gap' in the Pyrenees had been closed by the reacquisition of Cerdagne and Roussillon in 1659.

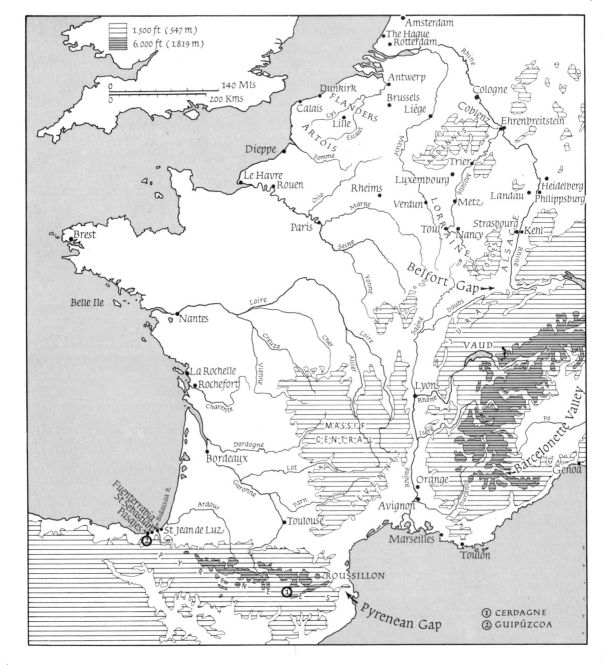

The progress of 1658 went through Burgundy and the Rhône valley to Lyons, and the route back to Paris was purposely chosen so that the King might see, and be seen in, other parts of central France. The south-west and the south were visited in 1659 and 1660 when the court spent more than a year away from Paris, in connection with Louis' marriage to Maria Teresa. The route chosen was over Chambord to Bayonne. From there many towns were visited, Avignon, Montpellier and Nîmes among them. There was plenty of time, since Louis' marriage to Maria Teresa, originally fixed for February 1660, was postponed – so that her trousseau might be fittingly splendid – till June. Care was taken to show the King in his power to former *frondeur* strongholds like Bordeaux and Marseilles; at the latter place – where Louis XIV inspected the galley-fleet and saw the Mediterranean for the first time – a symbolic breaching of the walls took place to signify the town's subjection to the crown. After the wedding in Saint-Jean-de-Luz the progress went via Bordeaux, Poitiers, Richelieu, Amboise, Chambord and Orléans to the castle of Vincennes, where the royal couple stayed a month, permitting preparations for the festive entry into Paris, set for 26 August, to go ahead.

Louis' later journeys inside France were – apart from hunting and holiday expeditions to royal and noble palaces, and the visit to Nantes in August–September 1661 to meet the Estates of Britanny and be proclaimed king –

Table top of Louis XIV's reign showing the French provinces in 1684: the apogee of French expansion.

LOUIS' PROGRESSES
AND JOURNEYS

41

Louis at the manœuvres held at Camp de Coudon at Compiègne, 1698. On the left, the legitimized duc de Maine (without a hat), James II of England and Louis' eldest grandson (baton in hand), the duc de Bourgogne; immediately behind the King, the two younger grandsons, Philippe, duc d'Anjou and Charles, duc de Berri, and their father the Dauphin. The Dauphin was a good deal taller than Louis XIV, but he was usually so placed in paintings and engravings that this was not obtrusive.

related to war and defence, manœuvres and campaigns, the building of fortresses and the incorporation of new territories. In the War of Devolution he served in 1667 in the Spanish Netherlands as a cadet under Turenne and went in 1668 with Condé to invade and occupy Franche-Comté. During these campaigns he deepened knowledge gained in the 1650s of the northern provinces and covered new ground in the eastern areas of France; he also familiarized himself with places which later became French through conquest from Spain: he was present at the siege of Lille (ceded, with other towns in the Low Countries, in 1668) and had seen most of Franche-Comté (ceded in 1678). In the Dutch War (1672–78) the route, chosen for political reasons,* brought him know-ledge of yet another corner of France: from Charleroi along the Meuse until the territory of the bishopric of Liège was reached. It was here, from ground belonging to Louis' ally, the Archbishop-Elector of Cologne, that the Rhine was crossed and the Northern Netherlands invaded. The Dutch, who managed to stem the French advance, soon gained allies – the Emperor Leopold and Carlos II of Spain chief among them – and each new campaigning season meant travels through north-eastern or eastern France: Maestricht was success-

* By avoiding Spanish Netherlands territory it was hoped to preserve peace with Spain.

fully besieged in 1673 (though restored at the peace), Franche-Comté was conquered a second time and became officially French at the conference table at Nijmegen. The experience of eastern France, and of territories gained or secured by the Peace of 1678/79, was widened during the relatively peaceful years of the 1680s when Louis visited the fortifications and fortresses planned and built by Vauban to make a frontier as easily defensible as the one achieved by 1678 against the Spanish Netherlands.

During the Nine Years War (1688/9–97) Louis also travelled much. He was always present at the opening of the campaigning season and stayed with one army or another either till July (if things were going well), or till the very end (late September or early October) if there seemed any danger that France's enemies might succeed in invading the country. As he got older, however, his travelling tended to contract to the round between royal palaces. This was partly because his second, morganatic, wife disliked journeys and made him believe that too many of them were bad for him; but also because he now had, apart from the Dauphin and his two sons by Madame de Montespan, a second generation of legitimate royal princes – the dukes of Burgundy, Anjou and Berri, born in 1682, 1683 and 1686 respectively to the Dauphin from his marriage with Marie-Anne Victoria of Bavaria – to be used with the army and for other royal duties. His farewell to active soldiering may be seen at that great camp assembled for manœuvres at Compiègne in 1698 when these three grandsons, as well as his own three surviving sons, were in his suite. When the second of the grandsons, Philip of Anjou, journeyed south in 1701 to take possession of the Spanish crown left to him by the will of Carlos II, his grandfather said his goodbyes at Sceaux; it was the boy's tutors and courtiers, men of his father's generation, who accompanied Philip on his journey. And during the War of the Spanish Succession which followed (1702–13/14), Louis XIV, though still in command of the armed forces and in the closest contact by letter and meetings with his generals, did not visit the armies.

Philip's journey was nearly half a century in the future when Louis XIV as a young man of twenty-one travelled through France to Lyons in 1658. A young and gay party went with him, and the King, with no trace of the shyness so noticeable in his adolescence, was free and happy. Verbal descriptions of him at this, the springtime of his reign, are naturally flattering; but the brilliant blue-grey eyes, the fine mouth, the cleft chin, the naturally wavy hair, the measured grace and dignity when on duty, the great skill in dancing and in horsemanship, are beyond doubt. His delight in Marie Mancini's company was probably one reason for his happy spirits, though this was not yet guessed at by Queen Anne. He was so easy-going and chatty when he met his Savoyard cousin that his mother feared he was becoming infatuated with Marguerite and might commit himself to a marriage detrimental to her Spanish objective. This prospect, skilfully exploited by Mazarin and Lionne, secured Philip IV's agreement to give Louis his elder daughter for a bride. A messenger was dispatched to Lyons, and the Savoy and French courts parted with as much saving of respective faces as possible.

Louis seemed to give little heed to anything but the present. Yes, he dutifully echoed, Marguerite had been nice and he would have been willing to marry

Medal of Louis as a young man. Here we glimpse something of the charm which Marie Mancini recalled in her memoirs, as on the occasion when 'his Majesty, offering me his hand, and mine accidentally striking the pommel of his sword, I hurt myself a little: he quickly drew the sword from its sheath and threw it away . . . I cannot describe with what an air he did this, no words can convey it.'

MARIE MANCINI

43

her if that was his duty; yes, the prospect of a Spanish marriage was grander and Maria Teresa, from her portrait, looked more beautiful. But when he returned to Paris and the young companions of the progress took up their sweet and chivalrous round of amusements, in tune with the *précieuse* inclinations of Marie herself, he began to dread the parting from her. The romance became too obvious and the two were separated. Mazarin sent his niece to the west country, to Brouage, the old silted-up port near La Rochelle. Louis' hour-long interview with his mother, in which he failed to win her consent to his marriage to Marie, brought two concessions: he might bid her farewell and letters could pass between them. These, though unknown to the young lovers, were discreetly opened and read in transit. They showed that hope died hard: Louis promised Marie he would never marry anyone if he could not marry her; he hoped for a Spanish refusal of French peace terms, or for a change of heart in the Queen and Mazarin. The older couple began to fear that rumours of Louis' love for Marie would offend Philip IV's pride and cause him to break off both marriage and peace negotiations. It was high time to act. Mazarin's threats to leave France if Louis persisted in his plan had no effect, but a prolonged siege to the King's sense of duty and concern for his *gloire* carried the day. Mazarin played on many strings in those of his letters to Louis which have survived. At times he gently reminded Louis that in earlier years he had been willing to seek guidance on how to become a great king; at other times he laid down the law, 'God established kings to guarantee the property, the security, and the peace of their subjects, and not to sacrifice any of these for their own individual passions.... 'Even though you are master in one sense... you must account to God for your actions, for your own salvation, and to the world for the maintenance of your *gloire* and your reputation....It is not a question of your desires... your subjects' welfare and your kingdom are at stake.' The Cardinal knew precisely where to place the *coup de grâce*, 'Let me assure you that the Prince of Condé and others are alert to see what will happen...they hope to profit by any plausible excuse you may give them.'

Louis gave in, but persuaded the Queen to let him see Marie Mancini to explain his position. They met on 13 August at the town of Saint-Jean-d'Angély. The meeting made their grief harder to bear, and their letters continued. Louis always found it hard to go back on a promise, since a king's *gloire* was involved in keeping his word, and not until Marie broke off the correspondence in September 1659 did his letters to her cease. Mazarin, busily engaged in putting the final polish to the negotiations with Luis de Haro, was greatly relieved that his niece had let Louis extricate himself from the maze of love to follow the path of duty. He spared a thought for her sorrow: read Seneca, he counselled, he will console you.

Some historians have ventured a guess that if Louis had been permitted to wed Marie Mancini he would have been a happier and better man. There is no way of telling, but the fact that they met when both were married and the King seemed genuinely indifferent to her shows that the romantic love lost was a remembered, not a present sorrow. The sweet and physically consummated love for Louise de La Vallière was probably a greater milestone in Louis' personal life: the seduction of the senses in the summer of 1661 at Fontainebleau.

Opposite: *Peace of the Pyrenees.* Don Luis de Haro, the Spanish negotiator, is seen against the background of the Bidassoa river and the Island of Pheasants which formed the boundary between Spain and France. The ingenious arrangement on the island, whereby negotiations could be conducted without either Haro or Mazarin (and their suites) leaving the territory of their respective rulers, is clearly illustrated. A special conference chamber was constructed (see centre of the courtyard): its doors were so arranged and a table so placed that Philip IV's ministers and officials, as those of Louis XIV, remained on the 'right' side of their own frontier.

Gobelin tapestry representing the meeting of Louis XIV and Philip IV and their families on the Island of Pheasants. The conference chamber has been richly decorated with carpets, tapestries and hangings; but note that the frontier is emphasized by the very contrasting carpets beneath the feet of the French party and the Spanish one. The differences in fashion of the two courts can also be observed. On the Spanish side we note the Infanta Maria Teresa immediately behind her father, and among the courtiers Velazquez. On the French side Philippe is immediately behind Louis XIV and beside him are the Queen-Mother and Mazarin.

That Louis continued to be attracted to lively, quick-witted and well-read women is witnessed both by his most passionate love-affair, that with Mme de Montespan, and by his settling down with Mme de Maintenon in 1684. An ear for music delighted him; he and his sister-in-law Henrietta sang, played and danced together with enough pleasure to attract censure; Louise de La Vallière used to sing for him, while he accompanied her on the guitar, in the little house he gave her in the grounds of the Palais Royal. Mme de Maintenon also was an accomplished singer.

Louis' wife did not displease him when he first saw her. On 4 June, two days after the marriage ceremony by proxy in San Sebastian, he (having crossed incognito into Spain) was permitted a glimpse of her – through an open door into a room in Fuentarrabia where his mother and brother were conversing with Philip IV and his daughter: she was young, small, blonde and had clear blue eyes. On 7 June the French royal family welcomed the bride on French soil. Pictures now in the Prado depict the processions of the two courts; Gobelin tapestries, now in the Elysée palace, commemorate the meeting and the wedding which took place two days later. Maria Teresa was pliable and passionate by nature. She adored her husband and it was a great sorrow to her when he took mistresses. But she was not strong; she felt unwell when pregnant, had difficult labours and of the six children born to her and Louis only one, the first-born boy, survived.* It used to be believed that she was stupid and therefore bored her husband. Recent research has proved her better educated and read than was previously thought, and the explanation for Louis' finding her indifferent company must be sought elsewhere. She did not share his interest in sports and games and was possibly too devout and too docile for him. More important, she did not share his delight in the French language and could not amuse and divert him by discussing the latest play or poem or the latest witticism: indeed, her knowledge of French remained rudimentary. Louis certainly resented the fact that she ran to his mother, her aunt, for comfort. It was as if the two Spaniards were silently (and in his mother's case not always silently) upbraiding him and making him feel guilty over the mistress he had taken during his wife's first pregnancy, the young Louise de La Vallière. From this love-affair, which lasted six years (though Louise was not permitted to leave the court till 1674) four children were born.

Relief of Maria Teresa by Coysevox. This was placed in the Basilica of St Denis, the burial place for French kings and their consorts. The treatment is realistic and shows the Queen in early middle age. The double chin was partly a family trait and partly explicable by her fondness for chocolate and rich sauces. Lack of exercise also contributed to her plumpness.

To Louis and the French at large there was nothing reprehensible or new in the king's having mistresses and illegitimate children. If the mistress was introduced to the court, she became, as did Louise de La Vallière, a *maîtresse en titre*, and illegitimate children who were recognized were brought up at court as part of the royal family. From his earliest days Louis had been familiar with the fact that famous families had sprung from the bastard children of his ancestors; and members of the house of Vendôme, descendants of his grandfather Henri IV from the wrong side of the blanket, were well known to him. The very palace

* The others were: Anne Elisabeth (18.11.1662 to 3.12.1662), Marie Anne (16.11.1664 to 26.12.1664), Marie Thérèse (21.1.1667 to 1.3.1672), Philippe, duc d'Anjou (5.8.1668 to 10.7.1671), Louis-François (14.6.1672 to 4.11.1672).

La Chasse Royale de Chambor.
Pendant que la saison, Vous offre ses delices,
Et que le Ciel benin flatte vos tendres Ans,
Princesse, avec plaisir goustés ces exercices,
L'un et l'autre aussi bien ne dure pas long temps.

A Paris chez Lenfant rue S.Iacque avec privilege
le Potre del.

which was the setting for his and Louise's love proudly displayed in its decorations the intertwined ciphers of Henri and Gabrielle d'Estrées, of François I and Anne d'Etampes. In his Instructions for the Dauphin he took it for granted that kings had mistresses and was open about himself, warning his son only to guard against their gaining influence on policy.

There was, therefore, no moral problem for Louis in respect of his first mistress, though the disapproval of his mother (and his emotional attachment to her) caused him to postpone recognition of Louise as *maîtresse en titre* till after Anne's death in 1666. The children born to them before that date were kept discreetly away from court, brought up by Mme Colbert; after legitimization they became part of the royal household but – as they had no right of succession – without the appelation *enfants de France*. Grave problems arose, however, in

An Exhortation to the Young Queen. Anon. engraving with a verse advising Maria Teresa to enjoy the pleasures of the hunting season at Chambord in the Loire valley.

LOUIS' MISTRESSES
AND NATURAL CHILDREN

49

respect of Louis' relationship to Mme de Montespan. The fact that she was a married woman spelt double adultery and brought severe criticism on religious grounds. Considerable pressure was put on the King to break off the affair. This he was unwilling to do, preferring not to take holy communion at Easter (to 'do his Easter duty', as the contemporary phrase ran) once it became clear that a promise to give up Athénaïs was demanded before he could receive absolution. The Paris Parlement was petitioned for a legal separation of Mme de Montespan from her husband so that the double adultery might cease. Its lawyers were in no hurry and, in spite of Louis' repeated reminders, the decree took five years to materialize. Not till 1673 could the children of this union be recognized.

To avoid giving scandal, Louise de La Vallière retained her title of *maîtresse* long after she had ceded her place in the King's affection to her friend Athénaïs. Nobody was deceived. Fêtes with their allegorical plays, ballets, poems and fireworks contained sufficient allusions for the reigning mistress to be identified. The identification spread through popular ditties and general gossip; during royal progresses when both Louise and Athénaïs were bidden to travel in Maria Teresa's coach, while Louis accompanied them on horseback, those who watched the cavalcade pass would comment that they had now seen the extraordinary sight of 'three Queens in one day'.

That Louis should choose his mistresses from his wife's or his sister-in-law's ladies-in-waiting is not surprising: they were the women he had the most frequent opportunities to meet. What is surprising, and says much for Louise's generosity of spirit, is that she and Athénaïs remained friends. It was among the same court circle that Louis picked the fairly numerous mistresses of the late 1670s when his love for Athénaïs had run its course and before Mme de Maintenon had convinced him that he must, for the sake of his immortal soul, give up sinful pleasures and stay faithful to his wife. We are often told that the scandal of the 'poisoning affair', which rocked Paris and Versailles between 1680 and 1682, ended Louis' love for Mme de Montespan, though some variants have it that the love remained though the King was forced to break with one who was guilty of buying love-philtres, if not poison, and of saying black masses, or at least of having them said on her behalf. It is clear, however, that Montespan was not involved with any of the motley crew of fortune-tellers, abortionists, providers of poison and of occult ceremonies, arrested and examined by the special tribunal, the *Chambre Ardente*.

It is also known that Louis became promiscuous as early as 1676 when Athénaïs was pregnant with Françoise-Marie, Mlle de Blois, and that her love-affair with Louis came to a definitive end during the pregnancy of the seventh and last child she bore him in 1678. Athénaïs' very fecundity (she had already two children by her husband) counted against her. Louis was fond of children, but found women in the later stages of pregnancy less interesting and amusing than usual; it is symptomatic that Louise became his mistress in July 1661 when Maria Teresa was five months pregnant with the Dauphin, and that his affair with Athénaïs began in the summer of 1667 when the King, the Queen and her ladies, among them Montespan, went to the Low Countries while a heavily pregnant Louise was sent home.

The hunted stag. Sculpture at Versailles of one of the many sports enjoyed by Louis XIV.

Opposite: Louise de La Vallière portrayed as Diana, goddess of the hunt. Her prowess as a rider and her love of outdoor exercise had first brought her to Louis' attention when they met in April 1661. She bore him four children in the six years their love affair lasted, though only one, Marie-Anne, grew to maturity. Louise retired from court in 1674 and became a Carmelite nun.

Opposite: Athénaïs de Montespan
and four of her children by Louis
XIV. She worked hard, and intelli-
gently, to please the king. She dressed
in French lace and rich materials of
home manufacture as an advertise-
ment for France; she had three ships
built for him with her own money
and spent the large sums he gave her
in building the beautiful château
of Clagny which, with its fine decorations and pleasant grounds, gave
Louis much pleasure. Nor did she
neglect her looks as long as their
love affair lasted; she dyed her hair
blonde at one time to emulate
Louise de La Vallière's colour; and
in 1675 when Louis was absent on
campaign she took the opportunity
to diet at a spa, returning to court,
according to Mme de Sévigné, 'half
her size'. After their break she
became fat: an Italian diplomat
swore he had seen her upper leg (as
she entered a carriage) and that its
circumference was that of his own
waist.

Athénaïs, as she began to lose her figure, worried about losing the King.
She had two characteristics in common with the Queen; she was addicted to
gambling and she was jealous by nature, but unfortunately she was neither
submissive enough nor wise enough to hide her resentment of the King's
growing friendship (which did not at this time amount to love) with her own
old friend, Françoise Scarron, Mme de Maintenon. Fear was mixed with resentment, for Athénaïs' position would be undermined if Louis took Françoise's sermons seriously and decided to 'keep to the Queen alone'. Annoyance
also played its part. Had she not given Françoise Scarron, widowed and poor,
her chance of security by persuading the King to put their first-born children*

* She took charge of only the first two: a girl, born in 1669, who died young, and
Louis-Auguste, born in 1670 and created duc de Maine on legitimization. The
younger children were brought up by Mme de Louvois.

52

into her charge? Was it not Louis' generous rewards for that service which had enabled Françoise to buy the estate of Maintenon and live at court as the Marquise de Maintenon? The two women quarrelled and Louis, much against his inclinations, was drawn into their disagreements. He blamed Athénaïs for disturbing his domestic peace at a time when he had difficult problems of state to cope with, but unless there had already been an element of satiety in their relationship he would not have allocated to her the major share of the blame nor would he have been so easily tempted into a search for younger, attractive and cheerful partners.

Louis' succession of mistresses between 1676 and 1680 to some extent reconciled Athénaïs and Françoise in shared dislike of the present favourite: Françoise mortified at each new mistress because the King had not followed her advice, Athénaïs hoping, from the very frequency with which Louis changed mistresses, that he would eventually return to her bed. None of the affairs of this period proved of long duration, though the last, with the nineteen-year-old Mlle de Fontanges, 'beautiful as an angel', might have done so but for the fact that she fell ill and was no longer the gay outdoor girl Louis had appreciated: in her horsemanship she had nearly, but not quite, equalled Louise de La Vallière when young. Her illness had manifested itself after the birth of a stillborn child, and it is worth noting that Louis had no children, or at least none he wished to acknowledge, by any of the transient mistresses. Athénaïs' hope was not fulfilled. She remained at court until 1691 but though Louis visited her apartments every day, he took care never to be left alone with her. In 1691 Athénaïs, like Louise before her, took refuge in a convent, though unlike Louise she did not enter a religious order.

Two engravings by Robert Nanteuil, the second of which shows lines of tiredness and even of *ennui*. They illustrate the deterioration in Louis' looks between 1668 – the date of the portrait above – and 1676, the date of the portrait to the right. The disorders in his personal life in the 1670s may have contributed to this, but the setbacks of the Dutch war were probably of greater importance. We know that Louis tended to discontinue his military memoirs when things went wrong and, on restarting them, he managed to slur over (possibly without fully realizing what he was doing) happenings which might detract from his military *gloire*.

The victory went to Mme de Maintenon. Louis, shaken by the death of Mlle de Fontanges, decided to settle down. He returned to his wife, while relying on Françoise for company and conversation. She was three years older than he, but still attractive, intelligent as well as pious, busy with a school she had started, well-read and entertaining, though not witty in the way of the Montespan family. They had a strong bond in common: love for the elder boy, Louis-Auguste, of his union with Athénaïs. Louis found he could pour out to Françoise the things that bothered or worried him: the fear that the boy's foot, lamed by poliomyelitis, would not mend; the vexations of the day; the problems of his family and his responsibilities in general; and concern, off and on, for the salvation of his soul. The slightly teasing pet-name he gave her, *Votre Soliditée*,* speaks of the comfort and strength he received from her, though it has often misled historians into thinking Maintenon more steadfast in opinions and

* Mme de Maintenon wrapped up well (becoming 'solid') to protect herself against the King's habit of opening windows wide. Teasing, getting at her obvious piety, is also implied in Louis' occasional reference to her as 'la Sainte Françoise'.

LOUIS' SECOND (MORGANATIC) WIFE
Portrait by Mignard of Madame de Maintenon. The hourglass and the book hint at the serious side of her character. Louis, who kept their morganatic marriage secret, was, however, jealous of her honour (cf. p. 74), and the fact that her grandfather, Agrippa d'Aubigné, had been a companion-in-arms and close friend of his own grandfather, Henri IV, raised her in his estimation above the modest social position which was hers at court. He worried about what would happen to her after his death; in his will he asked that his successor should continue to support St Cyr, to which she retired and lived till her death in 1719.

Le Duc de Guise Roy Ameriquain

friendships than she really was. It has been assumed that they became lovers in 1681, but this seems unlikely. On her own evidence Françoise was frigid by temperament. She may or may not have been a virgin, in spite of her marriage to the poet Paul Scarron in the last, invalid, years of his life; but the way she refers in her letters to the distasteful duties which marriage brings to women makes it clear that for her these duties held no pleasure. It is highly probable that she made a morganatic marriage the price of her favours, giving the King a sufficiently strong hint when, after the Queen's death in 1683, she asked leave to retire to her estate since it would no longer be fitting for her to remain at court. Her correspondence with her brother at this time is full of excitement and hints at a wonderful honour and a high position within her reach; it also conveys that the King gave in to her conditions. The date of the marriage is not known (some historians put it in October 1683, others in June 1684, and even as late a date as 1697 has been put forward), nor was it ever made public. Her position was accepted in the family circle and signified by the fact that she remained seated in the presence of the King's children and grandchildren, legitimate and legitimized.

Louis had a great liking for children, his own and those of others. He enjoyed standing godfather to those whose parents he wished to raise in esteem: to playwrights like Molière who were looked down on by many of high rank; to ministers and officials who had served him well and whose marriages into older noble families he had promoted. He grieved when those of his children died whom he and his wife had hoped to rear: at the death in 1671 of their second son, Philippe, duc d'Anjou, nearly three years old, and at the death of little Marie Thérèse in 1672, just five years old. Two other daughters and one son died so young that they were hardly known to him, a fate kings shared with subjects. Statistically expressed, of the average brood of five children, two to three reached maturity in the seventeenth and early eighteenth centuries; Marie Teresa and Louis were thus less lucky than most in rearing only the Dauphin. Of his illegitimate children several died in infancy or when very young; two legitimized sons died in their teens. Of Louise's four children only one, Marie-Anne (the first Mlle de Blois, born in 1666), survived childhood; of Athénaïs' seven, four survived: Louis-Auguste, duc de Maine (born in 1670), Louise-Françoise, Mlle de Nantes (born in 1672), Marie-Françoise (the second Mlle de Blois, born in 1676) and Louis Alexandre, comte de Toulouse (born in 1678). As adults they often gave Louis trouble; but by that time the Dauphin's sons and grandsons filled him with joy, both personal and dynastic. During the birth of the Dauphin, Louis had held his wife's hand throughout the protracted labour. In his honour the most splendid of carousels was given in Paris in 1662, with riders dressed in magnificent costumes as historical and mythological figures. When the Dauphin's wife in her turn had a long and difficult labour, her life and that of the child being despaired of at times, the King, who had fed her with his own hand, was visibly moved as he announced the traditional 'We have a prince.' That his joy in children was more than dynastic, that he so to speak liked children in the abstract and the very concept of children, comes across in his order to sculptors charged with decorating Versailles and its park: *toujours les enfants.*

Opposite: The duc de Guise as 'an American prince' at the carousel, seen by 10,000 spectators, to celebrate the birth of the Dauphin.

The child as symbol: Puget's *Enfant et Dauphin.*
Below: a naturalistic image: *putto* at Versailles.

Busts by Coysevox of Louis XIV in middle age and the Dauphin as a young man. Note the sun symbol for Louis and the dolphin at the base of his son's bust.

It is evident from many incidents reliably reported that Louis had a way with children. A contrast usually drawn between his treatment of the Dauphin and the rest is not tenable for the childhood years. Nothing could be more psycho-logically right than Louis' answer to the Dauphin when he, as a boy of four, asked that a soldier who had not raised his hat to him should be punished. Not at all, the father explained, the soldier had done his duty and raised his halberd when the royal family passed by: he could not at one and the same time present arms and raise his hat. And the Instructions which he dictated (and in part wrote and corrected) in the Dauphin's first ten years are – as are many of Louis' precepts to those he charged with the boy's education – full of common sense. He was, however, conscious enough of the shortcomings of his own early schooling to overcompensate for his son, and the teachers he chose, Bossuet among them, were not psychologically suited to be in charge of a small child: the Dauphin came to dislike booklearning. The King did not fully realize what was happening and was himself guilty at times of believing that his son could be bullied into becoming an *honnête homme*. He was aware that the Dauphin was shyer, more in awe of him, and less good looking and lively than the Montespan children who were well coached in amusing and pleasing him, but his concern was always greatest for the Dauphin, the only *enfant de France* of his own body. As the boy grew out of adolescence Louis tried hard to build up his self-confidence. The recurrent themes when the Dauphin par-ticipated in campaigns were: do not risk your life needlessly; France needs you; you have done enough for your *gloire*; I am well satisfied with you. They shared many interests: the Dauphin was an intrepid hunter, fond of music, and a keen collector of art – a taste encouraged by Louis who, on his son's twentieth birthday, presented him with 50,000 *écus* 'to buy pictures'.

The favourite of the 1670s, Louis-Auguste, also went to war. Though he was not the coward depicted by Saint-Simon, his military gifts were insufficient to smother the rumours of ineptitude maliciously spread by those at court who resented the bastards. The other Montespan son, the comte de Toulouse, gave greater cause for pride; he applied himself to his career in the navy and showed valour and initiative in the battle of Malaga in 1705. Both boys married well, and the three illegitimate daughters, thanks to the large dowries the King gave them, found princes of the blood as bridegrooms. Marie-Anne, Louise's girl, married Louis-Armand de Bourbon, prince de Conti, who died when she was still only nineteen years old. She was in love all her life with his younger brother, François-Louis de Bourbon (prince de Conti on her husband's death), and they had a discreet but happy affair as long as he lived; she was very attached to her half-brother the Dauphin and accompanied him to functions in which his second (morganatic) wife could not take part. Of Athénaïs' daughters by Louis, the elder, Louise-Françoise, married Louis III de Bourbon, prince de Condé, a marriage that brought prestige, though it was not a happy one. Françoise-Marie, the younger, did best of all with her marriage to the King's legitimate nephew, Philippe, duc de Chartres (and duc d'Orléans on his father's death in 1701). His mother, Liselotte, raged that the quarterings of her son's descendants should be spoilt by his marriage to a bastard whose mother was without a drop of royal blood. Much later, when a daughter of this union was married to Louis' legitimate grandson, the duc de Berri, Liselotte was overjoyed. Berri was a favourite of hers and the marriage made her beloved Philippe the father-in-law of a legitimate descendant of Louis XIV.

'The Bastards': Louis XIV's legitimized sons who reached maturity were known by their enemies at court by this soubriquet. To the left, Louis-Auguste, duc de Maine; to the right, Louis-Alexandre, comte de Toulouse.

The third generation. The eldest grandson, the duc de Bourgogne, with his wife Marie-Adélaïde of Savoy and his two younger brothers; he points to a portrait of the Dauphin. A portrait of Louis XIV is on the wall.

Below: Marie-Adélaïde sculpted by Coysevox as Diana, goddess of the hunt. A bust of her by the same sculptor is in Louis XIV's bedchamber at Versailles; one of the few furnishings which we know for certain was there in Louis' lifetime.

Opposite: *The survivor of the fourth generation.* Little Louis, dauphin after 1712, is here depicted at his lessons being visited by the King. Note the library through the open door and the mathematical and scientific instruments in the foreground.

Three sons who survived of the marriage between the Dauphin and the Bavarian princess were all the objects of the King's close concern: the air they breathed had to be fresh, their nurses had to be pretty, their education of the best. In their late middle age, Louis and Mme de Maintenon shared a delight in the high spirits of Marie-Adélaïde of Savoy, the bride – not yet twelve years old when she arrived at court in 1696 – of the eldest of the grandsons, the duc de Bourgogne. Until the marriage was consummated in 1699 she lived as a child with them, spoilt but affectionate, and went to school at Saint-Cyr. She remained the King's favourite relative all her life. It was through one of her sons (born in 1710 and named Louis) that the dynasty survived in the direct line. The Dauphin for whom it had been prophesied that he, the son of a king, should also be the father of a king,* though never king himself, died of smallpox in 1711; a virulent form of measles or a kind of bubonic plague in the next year killed both Marie-Adélaïde, her husband and their elder son; in 1714 the duc de Berri died after a fall from his horse. Only the little Louis remained. There is a faded, touching picture, now in the Musée Carnavalet, of Louis XIV in the last year of his life visiting his five-year-old great-grandson in his schoolroom, directing his attention to maps, charts and a globe of the world.

* His son Philippe, duc d'Anjou, became king of Spain in 1700 as Felipe V.

60

When Mazarin died on 9 March 1661 the time had come for Louis to enter the world of politics on his own. The minister, ailing with cancer, had led the King's thoughts in the direction of personal government and had put aside, so Colbert divulged, some 5 million *livres* to facilitate such independence. Louis certainly behaved as if he had prepared for the moment, giving immediate orders that henceforth he alone would authorize action, that all petitions (*placets*) be put before him and that no money be spent without his knowledge. He discontinued the big council. Three experienced administrators formed the nucleus of his governmental advisers: Le Tellier for military affairs; Lionne, the foreign policy expert, and Fouquet, in charge of the finances and also Attorney General. Fouquet's position was far from secure in this *Triade*. Mazarin had warned the King against Fouquet in the same breath as he had recommended Colbert. Louis began a secret investigation of Fouquet's accounts. The figures which the *Surintendant* gave him in afternoon sessions he checked in the evenings with Colbert, whom he had nominated Fouquet's assistant. Thus the two unravelled, in so far as possible, the financial state of France and the stratagems by which some subjects, and Fouquet in particular, had over the years grown rich and the crown poor.

The picture was, superficially viewed, a gloomy one. The crown's income for 1661 and 1662 and part of that for 1663 had been anticipated. The state debt stood at 11 million *livres* and no arrangements had been made for funding it or for paying it off in regular instalments. The tax which non-noble subjects paid, the *taille*, was so inefficiently collected that a deficit of 8 million *livres* was usual between the estimated amount and the sum handed over by the tax farmers. Recent harvests had been bad and the *taille*, the *gabelle* (the tax on salt) and the tithes to the Church burdened the peasants to the extent that wide-spread tax-riots threatened and unrest had to be suppressed by force in some places. The French coinage ranked low when compared with the Spanish *pistole* and the Dutch florin. The trade balance was unfavourable.

But France's resources were vast. However backward her technology and agriculture at this time, the sheer size of her territory, the fertility of her soil and the mass of her population – larger than in any single unified country in Europe, at least 15 million peasants and another 5 million who earned their living from income on land, from *rentes*, from trade and crafts, from the professions and administration and as urban workers – enabled her to prosper. As immediate palliatives the *taille* was lowered to still unrest and the army was cut to the bone to save money. Fouquet was given every opportunity to suggest reforms and admit to former irregularities; but he left confession too late. Slowly and carefully Louis prepared for Fouquet's arrest during the court's stay at Nantes in the late summer of 1661, having first induced him to sell his Attorney Generalship in order to minimize the risk of a parliamentary *Fronde*. Louis' tenseness, as well as his dependence on his mother's approval, is evident in the long letter in which he reported to her (with a hint also of pride at a job well done) every step he had taken to secure the arrest. The story that Louis toppled Fouquet out of spite, because a mere subject had dared to entertain him royally at Vaux-le-Vicomte – though still found in textbooks – is no longer taken seriously by professional historians. The danger to Louis,

the one he saw and was explicit about, was that a man as rich, ambitious and unscrupulous as Fouquet, with a private army on his estate at Belle-Ile, might hold the crown to ransom and become a minister who dictated the king's policy, preventing the reform work which Louis and the administrators he gathered round him thought necessary. The severity of Fouquet's punishment is a measure of Louis' fear. The *Surintendant's* judges, after a trial that lasted three years, found him guilty and suggested he be exiled for life. The King, using his prerogative, changed this to imprisonment in the French-Italian fortress of Pignerol.* Vaux-le-Vicomte was sold to pay the fines imposed in repayment of his frauds, Louis taking, in lieu of cash, many of its treasures, among them tapestries, statues, ornaments and 1,000 orange trees. The King's harshness towards a minister who was widely recognized as one of the most civilized men of the time, patron of the rising generation of artists and *savants*, shocked contemporaries. However just the royal sentence, what about royal benevolence and mercy?

When the reform and rebuilding work got under way, in all spheres of French life in the 1660s, Louis benefited not only from the bureaucratic experts trained by Mazarin – Colbert, who took Fouquet's place as Controller, pre-eminent among them – but also from architects, bibliophiles and painters encouraged and helped by Mazarin and Fouquet. The continuity in administration represented by Le Tellier was also significant, as was the custom by which the sale of posts, or of reversions of posts, enabled skilled administrators to train sons and other relatives in the knowledge that profitable office would remain in the family. Nobody, however, could become a member of Louis' small council of ministers by buying an office – those called to the *conseil d'en haut* were named by the King alone – but the opportunity to work well and be noticed was in the first place bought through family or other patronage. The administrative

Three of Louis' trusted ministers. Far left: Colbert, in the centre Louvois, next to him Torcy. Seventeen ministers in all served Louis in his *Conseil d'en haut*, a remarkably low number in view of the length of the reign.

MINISTERS
AND ADMINISTRATORS

* Fouquet, who died in 1680, was not the 'man in the iron mask' prisoner at Pignerol, whose identity has not been discovered.

families, of the *noblesse de la robe*, formed in Louis' reign a class of their own, the *gens de la plume* (better rendered perhaps as a *noblesse de la plume*). Though they intermarried with the *noblesse de l'epée* and even with *les grands*, they still thought in terms of administrative and governmental careers for their sons. They formed clans and connections, and Louis found it useful to balance the most important of them, the Colbert, the Le Tellier and the Phélypeaux families, particularly in the early years of the reign, against each other. With the growing bureaucratization of the government (by 1712, for instance, the Ministry of Marine had 10 bureaux), the head of such connections found it relatively easy to place bright and hardworking protégés. It says much both for their influence and for their hereditary ability that of the seventeen ministers Louis called to his council throughout his active reign (an astonishingly small number, given the length of the period 1661–1715), five were of the Colbert family, five of the Le Tellier connection and one a Phélypeaux. The remaining ministers were also administrators (Lionne, Pomponne, Chamillart, Voysin) with the exception of the duc de Beauvilliers, a courtier of the old nobility, and the marshal Villeroi, a career soldier. Though the *conseil d'en haut* was kept small, varying from three to five ministers at any one time, experts from the bureaucracy or from the armed forces were frequently called to attend particular meetings where their advice was required. So were, occasionally, those important members of the royal administration, the *intendants*, who early in the reign were transformed from the travelling inspectors of Richelieu's and Mazarin's times to permanent governorships of provinces, each kept in his post as long as possible to ensure knowledge in depth, though his commission could be revoked at the King's will.

REFORM AT HOME   The reform work of the 1660s was first and foremost directed towards economic and financial matters. France had been drained of money by war in Europe for nearly two decades and had also suffered dislocation of trade and crafts by the Huguenot rebellions of the 1620s and the *Frondes* of the 1640s and 1650s. The country had regressed if comparison were made with the two most important rivals for trade and overseas expansion, the Dutch and the English, who had been free from large-scale involvement in the Thirty Years War. France, potentially so prosperous, was lagging behind countries with far smaller populations but better organization and exploitation of resources. The measures taken to redress this state of affairs were intensive and have been positively evaluated in recent years by French economic and financial historians. Manufactures were revived and new ones introduced. The King's building programme at Versailles, as later at Marly, created opportunities for French manufactures – for Gobelins, for mirrors, for fine woven materials – and gave employment to numerous painters, sculptors and designers as well as to thousands of artisans for furniture, silver and interior decoration in general. The court-life of conspicuous consumption as far as clothes were concerned similarly created demands for lacemakers, tailors and embroiderers, for jewellers, bootmakers and hatters. Export was aimed at, both in Europe and overseas, and these new manufactures, especially clocks, fine textiles, lace and *objets d'art*, were added to the traditionally peasant-produced exports of salt, wine, brandy and coarse textiles.

A great many trading companies were founded; to these Louis contributed directly in money and indirectly by encouraging the nobility to engage actively in overseas trade: a nobleman would not, it was re-emphasized, forfeit his noble status if he became a trader. The needs of the army and navy also led to large-scale production of uniforms, weapons, guns and ships. With peace and a new regime came a will to work in the hope of harvesting the fruits of one's own industry. The population as a whole remained at the mercy of such catastrophes as successive bad harvests or epidemics of malaria, typhoid and the plague; but demographically speaking the losses were speedily made up, as was the loss of life incurred in war. Better methods of control ensured that more tax money, in spite of the *taille* being lowered, could be disposed of by the government, and in an amazingly short time confidence in the coin of the realm was restored at home, though the French *livre* always fluctuated in the international market and tended to fall considerably in times of war.

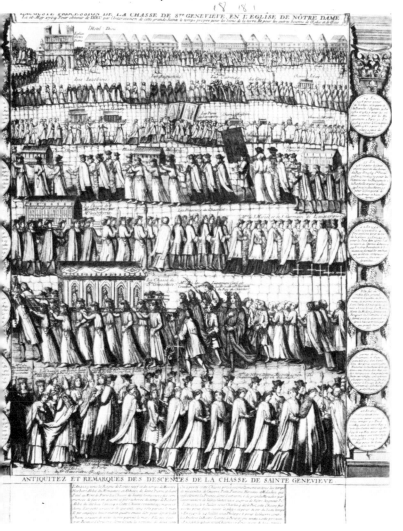

The terrible year. After two consecutive bad harvests and the cold winter of 1708–09, there was famine and distress throughout France. In Paris on 16 May 1709 the relic of Sainte Geneviève was carried in solemn procession from Notre Dame to implore God's help.

65

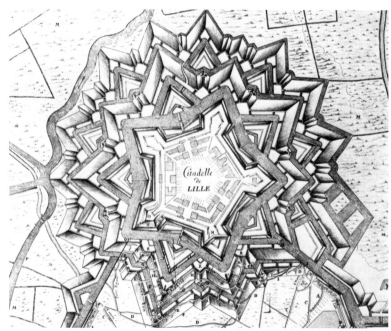

Guardsman. Study by Watteau.

The next step, which began simultaneously with the work to better the economic and financial situation and was, indeed, dependent on success in these areas, was to reform the army and to create a navy. Much preliminary work had already been done by Le Tellier regarding administration; it was now a matter of forging an army disciplined enough in the officer-class to make an effective instrument for the policies of the crown. The concept of the noble officer as the owner of his regiment had to be broken to prevent future *Frondes*: merit rather than noble rank must be made the basis for promotion and the training of future officers must be brought under central control. Not that Louis or his advisers were 'anti-noble'; indeed, the nobility was designated by the King as the class which, through its tradition of armed service and its *ethos*, was pre-eminently fitted as an officer-class. He insisted, however, that this alone did not fit the young nobleman for the new army: he would have to be trained to ensure cohesion and obedience and must learn to obey orders to fit him to give orders. At the same time Louis wished to be able to bestow high army rank on less well-born but deserving officers; one way to handle this problem in the transitional stages was for Louis himself, or a member of his family, to be in nominal command of an army so that high-born officers should not take umbrage at the very real command exercised by such a man as, for instance, Vauban.

In the early 1660s the army was kept small, for financial reasons, but it expanded – as did magazines for food and munitions – as tension with Spain over the Queen's rights grew. In the War of Devolution and in the Dutch War the army had a great many hired troops (one-third of an army of 120,000) but by the Nine Years War a mainly French army of 220,000 could be raised and in the War of the Spanish Succession, including the militia, some 350,000.

Général d'Armée.   Maréchal de France.   Lieutenant Général.   Colonel.   Lieutenant Colonel.

Major.   Capitaine.   Lieutenant.   Sous-Lieutenant.   Enseigne.

Sergent.   Caporal.   Anspessade.   Grenadier.   Mousquetaire.

Piquer.   Tambour.   Fifre.   Vivandier.   Goujat.

Ranks and uniforms of Louis XIV's army.

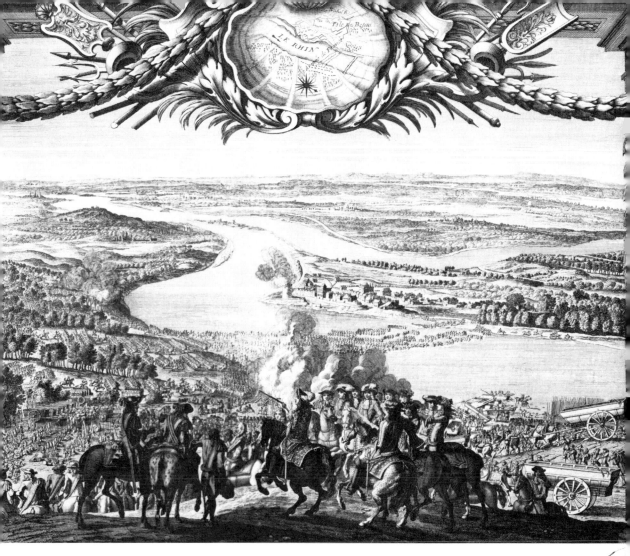

These large armies were, however, reduced at the end of hostilities, while the soldiers of the peace-time kernel were employed on such work as the building and improvement of fortresses, and helping with digging and construction for royal palaces. Some were billeted in towns and villages, especially in areas which had proved, or were deemed, restive; from this custom (intended to save the crown expense) developed the infamous *dragonnades* which put pressure on the French Protestants to return to the Catholic faith. Innovations in artillery and weapons date mainly from the 1680s and took place, partly as a consequence of tactical reforms in the European armies fighting the Turks, and partly as a result of lessons taught by France's enemies in the 1690s – at Steenkerk, for instance, Louis' soldiers won a victory which owed something to the fact that they grabbed the fusils of their dead enemies for quicker firing. French firing patterns remained, however, inferior to those of the Marlborough armies in the War of the Spanish Succession, a factor of considerable significance in the great battles of that war.

The crossing of the Rhine in 1672, preparatory to French invasion of the Dutch Republic. Note Louis with baton raised.

Opposite: Louis XIV as commander of the military forces. Painting by van der Meulen.

If the army was the work mainly of Le Tellier, his son Louvois, Martinet and Vauban, the navy was the responsibility of Colbert and his son Seignelay, and after his death Pontchartrain of the Phélypeaux family. Connected with the growth of the navy proper (from less than 20 seaworthy ships in 1661 to 60 men-of-war in 1667, 140 in 1677 and 230 by 1688) was the growth of the merchant marine which could, especially in the heavily armed East Indiamen, constitute a reserve in times of war. It was particularly significant that Colbert managed to place the affairs of the French colonies under the Ministry of the Marine: without such all-over control of the vital links of communication the colonies could not be promoted. Similarly, the way in which the merchant marine and the navy proper were administered facilitated the change to privateering warfare after 1692 and after 1704, when the combined navies of the English and the Dutch had proved too strong an adversary for that of France. In the French navy, officers with merchant shipping experience were as readily admitted as were officers specifically trained for it.

In addition to the sailed men-of-war, based on Brest and Toulon, a strong galley-fleet was created. This was mainly for use in the Mediterranean, primarily to protect the French port of Marseilles against North African pirates; but there was also a small galley-fleet stationed at Rochefort for use in western and north-western waters. It became increasingly difficult to man the galleys. Officers were fairly plentiful; galley slaves were scarce since the Christian-Islam naval conflicts in the Mediterranean had eased. There is a telling clause in the Second Partition Treaty (1700), which visualized Naples and Sicily and the Tuscan ports as the Dauphin's share of the Spanish heritage, stressing that the galley slaves of these territories should become his. Louis learnt about the navy in much the same way he had learnt, as a boy, about the army: by models. A miniature fleet, with every kind of ship in use, was built and sailed on the canal at Versailles and mock battles were staged. This flotilla, under the command of the marquis de Langeron, is perhaps less well known to posterity than the gondolas sent to Louis as a gift from the Republic of Venice and much used for evening excursions to music.

The merchant marine. Allegorical presentation.

Man of War. Study by Le Brun of the older type of decorated ship.

Opposite: *The privateers.* Captain Jean Bart against a background of the small, but fast-sailing privateering ships in action.

Louis' concern for and interest in the armed forces was equalled, if not surpassed, by his absorption in what we might call French intellectual and artistic life, though this was conceived of as having practical importance as well as aesthetic value. The King was in many ways an innovator, a fact which Voltaire wished to emphasize in his '*Non seulement il s'est fait de grandes choses sous son règne, mais c'est lui qui les faisait.*'

In the *Académie Française*, founded by Richelieu in 1635, Louis pressed for a more liberal interpretation of 'men of letters'. He insisted, successfully, that Racine and Boileau ought to be among its members, though his promotion of Molière did not result in election. The task with which the *Académie* had been entrusted, a dictionary of the French language, proceeded slowly and in 1663 Louis created the *Petite Académie des Inscriptions et Médailles*, with four members only, for matters of relative urgency: the wording of inscriptions for coins, medals and statues, the checking of verse and prose works dedicated to the King to ensure that they were worthy of the honour, and the organizing of frameworks for festivities to celebrate royal and state occasions. It would be easy to ridicule – as has been done – this Academy as an organ either of censorship or of Louis' glorification, but its real purpose was to raise the standard of the French language in official use, to ensure historical accuracy and to commission designs fitting the symbolism of the state as well as the royal preference for clarity. The magnificent medals of Louis XIV's reign owe a good deal to the work of the members of the *Petite Académie* who sought out fine medallists, such as Varin and Mauger, and picked Grandjean, the engraver, when an edition of the medals for the first part of the reign was printed in 1704. For this first edition (followed by others) a new typeface, sponsored by Jean Annisson, the typographer royal, was used which is still regarded as among the best of post-Renaissance founts, and the commentaries were written by Charpentier, Racine and Boileau.

Opposite: Detail of painting of a session in the Academy of Science. The work done under its auspices was important enough for Voltaire to argue that without Louis' patronage of astronomers, 'there could have been no Newton'.

Below: Medal by Mauger with inscription *Securitas Alsatiae* of 1699 (see p. 108). On the reverse, portrait of Louis XIV.

Censorship there was, but in the reports of censors which have survived (mainly from the later period of the reign) a concern for standards is more evident than suppression of criticism. Refusal to print a book had to be justified and the reasons given between 1699 and 1704, when Pontchartrain's nephew, the abbé Jean-Paul Bignon, head of the King's Library, coordinated the work of 56 expert readers, are various: some manuscripts were refused because they were judged 'too trivial', others because they were 'likely to promote superstition', one at least because it was 'immoral, in that it describes incestuous love between brother and sister'. Political considerations did, however, operate in this post-Revocation* period in that books considered inflammable from the religious point of view (whether they were too Gallican, too Jansenist or too Quietist) were not passed; neither were excessively outspoken satires on religion in general. On the whole, however, the criteria were scholarly and the King's orders that anything that was useful (*utile*) should be printed were obeyed. This is not to say that crude forms of censorship did not exist. A Lyons printer was hanged in 1694 for having produced and sold a libel on Mme de Maintenon which involved the King: he had depicted her late husband, Scarron, as a ghost haunting Françoise at Versailles, reproaching her for immoral conduct.

The emphasis on utility was strong also in the founding of the *Journal des Savants* in 1665; learned and practical men were asked to bend their minds to inventions and to discover processes useful for French manufactures. The *Académie des Sciences* of 1666 (with fifteen members, each paid 1,500 *livres* a year) encouraged French work in the natural sciences; and supported research in France of foreign scholars like the mathematician Huygens from the Dutch Republic, and the astronomers Cassini from Italy and Rømer from Denmark. The Academy also contributed greatly, as did successive Ministers of the Marine, to advances in cartography and hydrography. A more personal concern to support the arts in general can be noted in Louis' foundation of the Academy of Painting and Sculpture (1655), the French Academy in Rome (1666) and the Academy of Architecture (1671) since members of all three promoted the visual arts and building plans so important to the King. Again, financial support was not confined to Frenchmen, and was extended even to artists who did not work in or for France, though as the financial position became tighter in the later 1680s – a temporarily reduced tax-paying age-group (caused by pre-1661 demographic changes) coinciding with heavy and somewhat unexpected war expenses – any money that could be spared was spent at home, and even the building programmes at Versailles were halted.

Domestic problems loomed largest in the early years of Louis XIV's personal rule. As he reminisced in his Instructions to the Dauphin, everything looked so fair abroad (the treaties of Westphalia and of the Pyrenees having pacified Europe) that a young king thirsting for military glory might regret the

LOUIS IN EUROPE lack of opportunity to win it. The European situation, however, never remained stable, and since the position of France in Europe was, traditionally, the chief concern of its ruler, foreign affairs increasingly occupied Louis' time and energy, while four wars (1667–68, 1672–78/9, 1688/9–97, 1702–13/14) inter-

* For the revocation of the Edict of Nantes, see below, p. 92 f.

rupted reform work at home. The reason was not far to seek. France had extended northern and eastern borders which could easily be invaded – along the river valleys which led from Southern Netherlands and the lower Rhineland territory deep into France, through Lorraine and the Belfort gap in the Burgundy region, over the Savoy passes and Barcelonette further south. Problems could and did arise which were independent of France in their origins but which profoundly and immediately affected French strategic interests. In this respect Louis' foreign policy reactions may be labelled defensive in intent, even where war ensued. But the very recovery of France and the determination of Louis and his ministers to exploit France's resources created problems for other European powers. Louis' concern to strengthen his northern and eastern strategic position caused fear in his German neighbours; his drive to catch up with the Maritime Powers in trade and colonial ventures met with counter-measures. In this respect Louis' initiatives had aggressive implications which brought fear of France as an exorbitant power and became catalysts of war.

The experiences of Richelieu and Mazarin gave some guidelines, focusing attention on the Habsburg ring pressing round France with northern Italy as the point where contact could be broken; it was for this reason that Richelieu had stuck to Pignerol, which controlled the mountain passes of the Alpes Maritimes, and Louis continued this policy with the buying of Casale in 1681, from a bankrupt duke of Mantua. But Louis was faced with other urgent problems which resulted, when the dice were called, in the sacrifice of the north Italian position in order to safeguard France's eastern frontier, and the abandonment of control of or influence in the southern part of the Italian peninsula and its islands – even though one French man-of-war had defeated thirty-seven Spanish galleys off Elba in 1664, and Carlos II's will of 1700 had made Louis' grandson heir to all Spanish possessions, including those of Italy. For the same reason, the need to define priorities, Louis was by 1693 constrained to effect a compromise with the Papacy and modify the Gallican stand he had adopted in 1682. Increasingly Louis' concern was directed from Italy to two key issues: the defects of his northern and eastern frontiers and the expansion of French trade and colonization to supplement the income from land in a reign of fluctuating agricultural prices (which fell, especially for grain, whenever there was a good harvest) and a general slow decline in land-values.

The Peace of Westphalia had given France sovereignty over the bishoprics of Metz, Toul and Verdun so that these territories, long occupied and administered,* could be fully incorporated into France and their exact boundaries determined by that examination of charters and other documents in respect of 'dependencies' which was the normal concomitant of any cession of land – a lengthy process since the new owner naturally wanted to claim as much as the law entitled him to and the late owner was correspondingly reluctant to hand over more than he must. Work on ascertaining what disputed places (usually small, but of strategic significance) should come to France with the bishoprics started immediately after 1648, but the war-effort against Spain till 1659, the primacy of the reforms at home, and Louis' first two wars – both directed

The fortress of Pignerol in the Savoyard Alps which Louis sacrificed in 1696 to obtain peace in Italy.

* For their position, see above, p. 8.

northwards – postponed the major part of the 'reunion' programme till after the Peace of Nijmegen (1678/9) when the Habsburg and Imperial challenge of the settlement of 1648 had been successfully met.

This challenge had been thrown down in respect of Alsace even more than in respect of the bishoprics. In the Peace of Westphalia the Austrian Habsburgs and the Empire had ceded 'all rights, properties, domains, possessions and jurisdictions' in the city of Breisach (a key fortress conquered during the Thirty Years War by the French), in the landgravates of Upper and Lower Alsace and in the Sundgau, to the crown of France. Ten imperial cities, known collectively as the *Décapole*, were, however, ceded only in respect of 'provincial overlordship' – which need not encompass territorial possession. Here was the seed of future conflict. Should the term be held to reserve sovereign rights for the Empire, or should the final paragraph of the treaty (to the effect that 'nothing stated above shall in any way diminish the sovereign rights accorded to Louis XIV') decide the issue in favour of France?

Tension between France and the Emperor, though not between France and the Empire, had grown ever since the signing of the peace of 1648. By it Ferdinand III had pledged himself not to help Philip IV of Spain either directly or indirectly in his war with the French, but before long he sent troops to fight on the Spanish side in the Southern Netherlands. The Empire as a whole was tired of war, and the Rhine states – conscious of the danger courted by Vienna – formed a league to safeguard their own neutrality. Mazarin managed to have France accepted in the League of the Rhine, and, via the German members, a clause was inserted into the capitulation of the Emperor Leopold (who succeeded his father as ruler of the Austrian state in 1657 and was elected Emperor in July 1658) that he must refrain from supporting France's enemies with soldiers, arms or money. The League tended to disintegrate after the peace of 1659 and was not renewed in 1665 in spite of Louis' efforts to keep it in existence. In peacetime the Rhine states felt less need for an association which to some extent was anti-Austrian. Their own position inside the Empire was in any case protected by French and Swedish guarantees of that *Landeshoheit* which the individual princes had wrested from the Emperor, and Vienna remained a source from which rights and privileges could, as opportunity offered, be obtained. Such prizes were increasingly valued more highly than the money Louis XIV was able and willing to offer in subsidies and pensions.

More significantly, the war Louis started over his Queen's rights in 1667 was not popular in the Empire where it was argued that the King of France had gained enough by the 1659 peace and should therefore be willing to forgive and forget that his wife's dowry had not been paid. The French attack on the Spanish Netherlands alarmed the Archbishop-Elector of Trier in particular, and the French invasion of Franche-Comté caused general unease along the Rhine. The news that Spain, at the congress of Aix-la-Chapelle, had avoided cessions in the east and confined them to the westernmost part of the Spanish Netherlands was welcomed, but the seeds of suspicion of France had been sown. They began to sprout when Louis was seen to cast covetous eyes on Lorraine and ripened – to Leopold's benefit – after Louis' attack on the Dutch Republic in 1672.

It must be admitted that the first steps towards hostilities were taken by Leopold, from whom Louis had thought himself safe by virtue of a treaty of neutrality signed in 1671. When the Emperor persuaded the Archbishop-Elector of Trier in May 1673 to admit Austrian troops into his fortresses of Coblenz and Ehrenbreitstein, both commanding vital Rhine crossings, Louis' armies risked the turning of their flanks; and when Leopold proceeded to occupy Philippsburg – belonging to the bishop of Speyer – an assault on Alsace was assumed imminent. Louis' countermeasures were swift and by necessity aggressive: he occupied the *Décapole*, besieged and took the capital of Trier and prepared to attack Philippsburg. In consequence Leopold was able to unite the Germanies – even across religious divisions – against France, and the Empire declared war on Louis in May 1674. Some German states, such as Bavaria, retained their alliances with Louis, but the Archbishop-Elector of Cologne had to disguise his attachment to France and withdraw from the Dutch war, while the Elector of Brandenburg – who had Rhine territories and interests – came into the war on the Dutch side in 1675.

From now on, whatever German allies Louis managed to keep or gain in war-time, the reversal of the 1648 settlement became an Empire objective as

The War of the Queen's rights (War of Devolution). Louis XIV (on horse-back, far left) and Maria Teresa with her ladies-in-waiting enter the still-burning Douai in 1667.

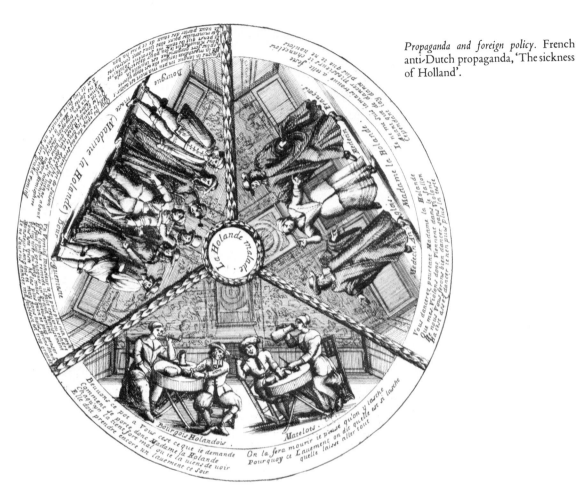

Propaganda and foreign policy. French anti-Dutch propaganda, 'The sickness of Holland'.

Dutch anti-French propaganda showing how 'pressed' the Republic was by Louis' aggression in 1672 and 1673.

well as an Austrian Habsburg one. From the invasions and ravages of Alsace in 1675 and in 1676–77 Louis, for his part, drew the conclusion that his overriding need was to close the gaps, the *portes d'entrée* on his eastern frontier. Propaganda by both sides, the French and the Dutch-German, was from now on constant and grew in volume as the English after 1688 were drawn into the anti-Louis camp. Learned treatises, subtle and less subtle pamphlets, witty plays, popular songs, especially soldiers' marching songs and drinking songs, scurrilous verses and crude cartoons accumulated and have survived in such numbers that they have proved likely to bedevil the work of historians who take into account only the output of one side or the other, or who are tempted to accept the arguments of either camp as gospel.

In the 'Dutch war' the French armies were successful enough (once they had rallied from the surprise escalation of the war), and Louis' diplomacy sufficiently skilled, to force the Peace of Nijmegen on the anti-French coalition. In it the Republic, which had been attacked by Louis, received compensation (*satisfactio*) by the sacrifice of Colbert's prohibitive tariff of 1667; while Spain, which had declared war on Louis, paid *satisfactio* in the form of Franche-Comté and eight places in the Spanish Netherlands. The *status quo* was restored in respect of Lorraine, the Emperor and the Empire, a great step forward since the French interpretation of 1648 had thus been upheld: Alsace, including the *Décapole*, was part of France. On top of this, Louis was permitted to keep Freiburg-im-Breisgau, conquered during the war by French forces. His offer to return it if only Philippsburg were given back to the bishop of Speyer was, however, spurned and Leopold's determination to keep this important key to Alsace in his own hands seemed a bad omen for the future. So was the Duke of Lorraine's decision not to return to his duchy: the restoration of the terms of the Peace of the Pyrenees (which his uncle Charles IV had accepted in 1659) seemed to Charles V humiliating and, even more so, the newly stipulated French occupation of Nancy and Longwy. He preferred exile in Austria, where he became viceroy of Tirol, married Leopold's sister, won fame as a general and bided his time for revenge. Meanwhile the French were left in occupation of Lorraine and Louis began to hope that sooner or later he would be in a position to offer the duke so tempting a territorial equivalent that this 'province of France' could be 'rejoined to the body and heart of the country'.

The gains of the 1678–79 peace were striking enough to make the French accord Louis the title *Le Grand*, but the King and his advisers were well aware of the weaknesses of France's position, especially in the east. In the north the newly won places permitted the building of a *barrière de fer*, planned and executed by Vauban. It consisted of fortresses linked by waterways and canals and proved strong enough, even when the 'lines' established in front of it were broken (as by Marlborough in the War of the Spanish Succession), to bar enemy invasion of France proper.

A similar defensive frontier was desired in the east where Spain had ceded Franche-Comté. The Rhine and the Moselle formed formidable barriers in themselves; but to nullify the Emperor's use of vital bridgeheads, a policy of 'reunions' was pursued between 1678 and 1681 which, by the examination of 'appurtenances and dependencies' in respect of new cessions and the continuation of such examination for the 1648 cessions, aimed either at linking French possessions or at controlling the foreign policy of princes who were made to accept French suzerainty through oaths of fealty, though their lands were not administered by France. The cornerstone of this system became Strassburg which, with its fortress Kehl (on the opposite side of the Rhine), was secured in 1681 not by a 'reunion' but by a mixture of threats and concessions as punishment for its recent cooperation with Frances' enemies: Louis XIV and Louvois stood close by with an army of 13,000 while terms which secured Strassburg's autonomy in domestic matters – including religious freedom, though at the price of handing the cathedral to the Roman Catholic Church – were negotiated. The loss of so important a free Imperial city embittered the Empire, and Louis' reunion policy inside Luxembourg, a duchy which, though Spanish, was an Imperial fief (and thus still part of the Empire), caused alarm. Louis discontinued his reunion policy in Luxembourg when the Turks attacked the Emperor in 1682, but on Spain's declaring war on him in 1683, a war provoked in part by pre-1682 French activities in the duchy of Luxembourg and the Southern Netherlands, the town and fortress of Luxembourg was conquered.

Carlos II had embarked upon this war hoping for military help from the powers that had signed treaties in 1681 and 1682 (the Dutch Republic, Sweden, the Emperor) with the objective of keeping France within the bounds of the Nijmegen Treaty. In the event, the first two powers proffered only diplomatic and financial support, while Leopold was too hard pressed by the Ottomans to enter the war, and Spain soon had to sue for peace. A truce for twenty years (the truce of Regensburg) was arranged in 1684 whereby the Emperor and the Empire, as well as Spain, agreed that France should, for that period, keep both German and Spanish 'reunions', the latter comprising – apart from Luxembourg – Courtrai and Dixmude in the Southern Netherlands. Louis hoped that France might, before the term ran out, find an opportunity to convert the truce into a permanent peace and a monument was planned for the eastern frontier with the proud inscription *Securitati Perpetuae*.

These words proved bolder than the facts warranted, and by the time the monument was raised on the banks of the Rhine in 1692, Louis was already – much against his will – involved in a new war with those German neighbours whom his minister Louvois had characterized already in 1684 as 'our real enemies'. The struggle which broke out in the winter of 1688–89 followed the by now familiar pattern of Leopoldian initiative and Ludovician countermeasures. With papal cooperation Leopold had in 1688 contrived to impose his own candidate, Prince Joseph-Clement of Bavaria, only seventeen years of age, as Archbishop-Elector of Cologne, though the French-sponsored coadjutor, William Egon von Fürstenberg, had been chosen by the majority of those entitled to elect Maximilian-Henry's successor. Appeals for arbitration in this matter as in that of a money compensation for Liselotte's inheritance in the Palatinate – debated since 1685 – were refused. Cologne was vital enough for Louis and Louvois to feel impelled to act, particularly as France wished at this time to create a diversion in the west to keep the Turks from making peace with Leopold. What the French King and his advisers had in mind, however, was a brief military campaign – say, of three months – which would forestall enemy invasion and, hopefully, transform the Regensburg truce into a permanent settlement. It developed into a Nine Years War.

This war marks a turning point in Franco-Austrian relations. In contrast to 1673, but along lines that were to be repeated in 1701–02, Leopold took the initiative even though there was no other war against Louis XIV in being – a fact that points to the growing self-confidence of Vienna after victories against the sultan in the 1680s. Secondly, the Imperialists moved fast (again a feature of the War of the Spanish Succession); already in October and November their troops were streaming towards the frontiers of France. Nor did Leopold have long to wait for allies outside the Empire, William III bringing both Maritime Powers into the war in 1689 and Spain joining this Grand Alliance in 1690.

During the Nine Years War, Louis realistically faced the distrust he had inspired in the Empire and in the Netherlands, and decided on a policy of rebuilding relations. He stuck to this in spite of vociferous French protests, in which street-ballads listed the victories of the war – Fleurus of 1690, Steenkerk of 1692, Neerwinden of 1694, and the successful sieges of Mons and Namur –

and compared them, line for line, with the reunions which Louis insisted on sacrificing at the peace congress of Ryswick. Conquered places were returned, and of the reunions only Strasbourg was kept. Lorraine was restored under conditions acceptable to Duke Leopold Joseph, and William III was recognized as King of England, though the Stuarts were not sent out of France as William desired: that would have been dishonourable. Louis would dearly have liked to hold on to Luxembourg, but he was anxious to improve his relations with Spain and it had to go.

LOUIS, THE EMPEROR AND THE TURKS

By this time Louis knew that he could never gain Leopold's friendship or even neutrality. This had become abundantly clear in the course of secret wartime negotiations with Vienna. Louis' offers to renounce his own and his heirs' claims on Spain and its empire, and to have such renunciations solemnly registered in the Parlement of Paris, were flatly refused, since Louis' price was a reaffirmation of the Peace of Nijmegen and an undertaking that Spain would not be united with the Austrian state under one and the same ruler. Leopold was not willing either to reaffirm the French interpretation of 1648 or to sacrifice his dream of re-establishing the multinational state of Charles V and persisted, by implication, in his German mission: Metz, Toul and Verdun as well as Alsace had to come back to the Empire. He also wished to retrieve Franche-Comté for Spain, though he was rather indifferent to the losses which Spain had sustained in the Southern Netherlands between 1659 and 1678.

In the event, Leopold's Dutch and English allies did not feel as strongly as the Emperor on this German mission – they were content to see the reunions restored – and though they had promised to support him in his claim to the whole Spanish inheritance, should Carlos II die while hostilities with France were in operation, this obligation came – in the view of the Maritime Powers – to an end with the Peace of Ryswick. Financially as exhausted as France, at least temporarily, William III and Heinsius, the Dutch Grand Pensionary, responded to Louis XIV's efforts to find a solution to the Spanish succession issue along lines of partition which would not disturb the balance of power in Europe and overseas.

These efforts eventually failed, and the English and the Dutch, as Leopold had predicted, chose – when the crucial moment came – to fight on the side of the Emperor in the War of the Spanish Succession. The Vienna and Rhine demand for a 'barrier' against France – by reversing the 1648 settlement – remained a principal objective throughout this war, but in its closing stages the Emperor Charles VI became so engrossed in Austrian objectives in Italy that the Empire accused him of putting the interests of his House before that of his German mission.

One other aspect of Louis' relationship to the Germanies needs to be noted. While the Austrian Habsburgs' chances of restoring the empire of Charles V remained in the balance (and was finally lost), Leopold was in the 1680s and 1690s making real gains in south-eastern Europe which, in Louis' judgment, endangered not only the French eastern frontier but the balance of power on the Continent. Victories over the Turks, though other princes participated (notably the Popes, the kings of Poland-Lithuania and the tsars of Muscovy), brought territorial aggrandizement mainly to the Emperor Leopold since

Opposite: Vase, in grounds of Versailles, still *in situ*, celebrating French participation in the defeat of the Turks at St Gotthard, 1664.

Greater Hungary as it was being reconquered from the Ottomans came, by historical right, into possession of the House of Austria. Louis XIV had little success in his propaganda campaign in the Empire and tried in vain to scare the princes with the spectre of an overmighty emperor who, in the wake of his Turkish successes, would make the Germanies into a *Monarchie*. The Vienna call of '*Auf, Auf Ihr Christen*' had the greater pull. From Austrian archive material we know, however, that Leopold was kept steadfast in his 'Christian mission' against the sultan by advisers who preached that only by a victorious conclusion in the east could he become strong enough to reverse the 1648 settlement in respect of France. Louis XIV's preoccupation with the Turkish issue in the 1680s was therefore not based on a chimera. Though he misjudged the domestic situation in the Empire, there was a real connection between Europe's crusade against the Ottomans and the safety (or otherwise) of his own eastern frontier.

The first phase of the Turkish onslaught, that of the early 1660s, did not pose any dilemma for Louis since his frontier problem had not yet become acute. Six thousand French troops helped to win the battle of St Gotthard in 1664 and Louis put soldiers and ships at the disposal of the Papacy for the defence of Candia (Crete), which ended in failure in 1669. Leopold, still childless, had not at this stage become intransigent on the Spanish succession issue and had in 1668 signed a secret partition treaty, recognizing his sisterinlaw's rights, with Louis. This promised France a fair share if Carlos II did not live to have heirs of his own body: the Spanish Netherlands, FrancheComté, Naples, Sicily and the Tuscan *presidii*, Navarre, the Philippines and the African ports, chief of which were Oran and Ceuta. Leopold's actions between 1673 and 1679 nullified this treaty and put Louis in a difficult position when the Turks recommenced their attack in 1682. *Raison d'état* dictated, first, a policy of noncooperation with the Emperor and, later, of active if secret encouragement of the Turks. Even so, Louis suffered from a divided conscience. He argued in public that he showed his solidarity with Europe's fight against the infidel by not attacking Leopold while he was preoccupied in the east. But for the King of France, known traditionally as *Rex Christianissimus*, to play so negative a part was galling, and the French historian Orcibal is undoubtedly right in attributing Louis' revocation of the Edict of Nantes (so contrary to his expressed and real desire to avoid force in religious matters) mainly to his need for a domestic crusade to cover up France's failure to act positively against the Turks.

Had Leopold and Louis been able to come to terms over the Spanish succession, this would still have left France in a conflictsituation of increasing severity regarding the Maritime Powers. Peaceful conditions after 1659 and Louis' domestic reforms released energies in commercial and industrial French life which led to harsh competition with the Dutch Republic and England on the Iberian peninsula, in the Mediterranean and, as French access to the western and southern seas began to be purposefully exploited, in the American, African and Far Eastern trade.

LOUIS AND THE DUTCH REPUBLIC

Clashes came first with the United Provinces. The Dutch were ancient allies, who yet resented the French gains of the Peace of the Pyrenees in the Spanish Netherlands and determined that Louis XIV's France must not come any closer: *Gaullus amicus, sed non vicinus.* During the Thirty Years War the Republic had fought ten campaigns to unite the ten provinces of the Southern Netherlands – in the initial revolt of 1568 against Spain as much part of the insurgent Netherlands as the seven northern provinces – with the North; but this was the work of the Princes of Orange, Stadholders of the Republic, rather than of the merchant oligarchy. When that oligarchy found itself in control, on the unexpected death of William II in 1650, for a long Stadholder-less period, it proved inimical to expansion: any extension of the territory of the Republic would make nonsense of the closing of the Scheldt and bring Antwerp into the fold – a competitor to the flourishing towns of the Province of Holland, Amsterdam and Rotterdam in particular, would emerge. The war-time plans for a division of the Southern Netherlands between the Dutch and the French (France to have French-speaking Artois and Flanders) were therefore abandoned.

Louis' war of the Queen's rights brought Franco-Dutch friction into the open. French historians have, so far without exception, classed this war – and the Dutch war that followed in 1672 – as 'defensive', while labelling the two later wars, the Nine Years War and the War of the Spanish Succession, 'aggressive'. Only the narrowest legalistic interpretation would, however, seem to justify even remotely Louis' application of Brabant private law, the *Jus Devolutionus*, to international relations in 1667. This law specified that a child of a first marriage was entitled to demand its inheritance, on the death of the father, before children of the second marriage; but it was not held by European contemporaries to give Louis licence to help himself, in Maria Teresa's name, to part of the Brabant. The Spanish lawyers refuted, promptly and convincingly, the legal reasoning of the French on this occasion. No justification at all seems possible for the premeditated attack on the Republic in 1672, well prepared diplomatically, though assurances were given to Sweden that the Republic would not be deprived of its 'international existence', i.e. it would not disappear from the map of Europe.

There is evidence that Louis, in later years, felt guilty about his aggression; a telling comment pleads the attack of 1672 as 'excusable' in a young and inexperienced king, flattered by fortune. Louis learnt from experience. The aftermath of the 1672 attack gave him a proper respect for the ability of William III, chosen as Stadholder to combat the French invasion, to fashion and hold together European alliances against France. The Southern Netherlands, Louis accepted from that day onwards, had to remain as a barrier, and the gains of Nijmegen from Spain were so arranged, by exchanges and equivalents, that lines of defence could be constructed and fortresses built to draw that square duelling field (the *pré carré*) which Vauban stipulated as essential to defend the northern frontier if it ever became necessary. Indeed, Vauban had, ever since 1668, explained to Louis XIV the weaknesses of the frontier obtained by the Aix-la-Chapelle peace, and there is evidence that the towns besieged and taken during the 1672–78 war were selected so that a proper defensive system could be built.

The hypothesis, admittedly based on slender but to this writer convincing evidence, that Louis in retrospect saw the error of his ways and, as in the Greek tragedies with which he was familiar, accepted the nemesis that pursued him as a just punishment, does not necessarily mean that there were not solid political and economic reasons behind the two aggressive ventures. The commercial rivalry between France and the Republic was expressed by the French protective tariffs of 1667 and the preferential duties aimed specifically at Dutch refined sugar in 1670–71, and in the Dutch retaliatory tariffs on French wines and brandies of 1671–72. More important was the French conviction that if the Republic was not willing to balance, even in the slightest degree, Dutch and French expansion into the Southern Netherlands – while still leaving a buffer state between them – they would have to be forced to accept at least the French right to expansion.

In the war of 1672 France had, at the outset, the Archbishop-Elector of Cologne and Charles II of England as allies; the first declaration of war on the Republic came from London, Louis' followed later. But English distrust of the French King, exemplar of the absolutist ruler, was such that within two years Parliament had forced a peace upon their king. In the event, Louis – who spent more money on subsidies and gratifications in England than in any other country – could not stem the three tides of constitutional, religious and commercial distrust towards his country from that of the Stuarts, either before or after the Glorious Revolution which brought William, the third Stadholder of that name in the Republic, to be the third king of that name in England.

LOUIS AND THE MARITIME POWERS The year 1688 tied the two Maritime Powers together in various ways and, ultimately, weakened the Republic in comparison with England. The larger population of England (Great Britain after the union with Scotland in 1707) had something to do with this, but William's initiative in overhauling the administration and the army of his kingdom, and his sacrifice of seniority for Dutch naval officers in joint fleet ventures made for a slow but sure advance of the English at the expense of the Dutch. The two nations had common interests: both were determined to limit French inroads on European, especially Spanish, commerce and to hinder development of and increases in France's overseas colonies and their trade, especially that in the Spanish empire. Indeed, the partition treaties,* whereby Louis and William between 1698 and 1700 tried to solve the Spanish succession problem, ultimately broke down because Louis was neither willing nor able to secure the Maritime Powers that share of the partition which they desired: safeguards for their commerce in the Mediterranean (Gibraltar, Port Mahon, Ceuta, and Oran were requested, and, though without much hope, Cadiz), in the West Indies and on the Spanish Main. Leopold proved (under pressure) more amenable and in the Grand Alliance of 1701 promised the Maritime Powers that they could keep 'everything' they were able to conquer in the West Indies.

Leopold, for all his theoretical intransigence against a partitioning of the Spanish empire while Carlos II was alive (after all, if the Emperor became an accessory to either the First or the Second Partition Treaty he might deprive

---

* Revision of the first treaty of October 1698 was necessitated by the death of its main beneficiary, Joseph Ferdinand of Bavaria, in February 1699; the second was signed in March 1700.

his House of the chance of being named sole beneficiary), was not unwilling to discuss partition after Carlos' death when the late king's will was found to have named Louis' second grandson the heir to all. The rub, however, was that the areas where the Emperor was willing to see Louis taking his share – the Spanish Netherlands and the Spanish empire overseas – were those in which the Maritime Powers would never tolerate a French presence, while those areas which William III and Heinsius were willing to consign to the Dauphin lay in Italy, where the Emperor was absolutely determined to reassert his position.

It is equally significant that Louis, in his negotiations with the Maritime Powers between 1698 and 1701, while unwilling to open European and overseas trading possibilities to the Maritime Powers – though obtaining for France the promise of the Spanish western maritime province of Guipúzcoa, rich in ports – did not intend to hold on to Italy. It was stipulated in a secret article of the second treaty that the duchy of Milan, part of the Dauphin's share, would be exchanged for either Lorraine or Savoy and Nice; and Louis made the greatest efforts (once the duke of Lorraine had signified his assent to give up his duchy for the Milanese) to persuade William III to let him exchange also Naples and Sicily for the whole territory of the duke of Savoy: Piedmont as well as Nice and Savoy. The French eastern frontier, from the north to the southernmost tip, would thus have been secured via the Spanish succession with the exception of Luxembourg, which William and the Dutch – much concerned with their barrier against France – firmly refused. William, initially opposed to the Naples and Sicily exchange scheme, was brought round when it became clear that English mercantile circles were opposed to the southern part of Italy becoming French. Negotiations were started for this second exchange but were overtaken by Carlos II's death and the revelation of his will.

The will put Louis in a dilemma. Should he stick to the partition treaty (though it was clear that the Maritime Powers would not, without further concessions, help to enforce this treaty on Leopold I) or accept the will – which precluded any partition – in its entirety? Only if he adopted the second alternative could he prevent that clause of the will being put into effect which stipulated an offer to Leopold in respect of his second son, the archduke Charles, if Louis should refuse, with – for good measure – an offer to a third candidate, Victor Amadeus of Savoy, if neither Louis nor Leopold proved willing to abide by the terms of the will. He chose the will, trusting that his sacrifices of the French gains stipulated in the Second Partition Treaty and the will's explicit prohibition against any future union of the undivided Spanish possessions with either France or the Austrian state would help to preserve the peace, and balance of power, in Europe.

Foreign policy problems of a weighty kind thus loomed large throughout Louis' reign. They were, in any event, those with which, because of the secrecy necessary in negotiations, rulers in all countries were particularly concerned; and in Louis' case they especially suited his temperament and gifts. He was prudent by nature, liked to speculate on the 'interests' of the European states and had a special affinity for negotiations built on meticulous and lengthy reports from a diplomatic corps which was better organized than most.

LOUIS' WORKING HABITS

Louis had a sustained capacity for hard work which made less inroads on his health than on the equally conscientious but more highly strung William III. Until Louis was past fifty he could cope with both work and play; after fifty, work tended to gain increasingly on play as he lost valued helpers of the older generation and before a new generation were fully trusted. Louis therefore spent his time according to a routine which hardly varied; but this cannot be guessed at from the gossipy accounts of Louis' life served up in the common run of textbooks and biographies in which an apparently aimless existence of *petit* and *grand lever* and *petit* and *grand coucher*, interspersed with other court functions of a ceremonial character, is depicted, the only relief being the time the King spent in the afternoon '*entre les draps*' (as court euphemism had it) with the mistress of the moment. Much is also made of the fact that he always bedded down with the Queen at night and of the one exception in 1667, at the beginning of the Montespan affair, when he kept his wife waiting till 4 a.m. and – challenged – blamed his tardiness on his paperwork.

Professional historians are apt to neglect Louis' personal world, in which mistresses and children, legitimate or otherwise, and physical exercise with horses and hounds, played an important role, since this part of Louis' life had no discernible effect on the King's domestic or foreign politics. This makes for as unbalanced a picture as the *histoire d'alcove*, and the specialist in any given field of the reign may thus miss clues to the total personality which have a bearing on wider issues. Where any specialist scores – through the examination of unprinted archive material and the analysis of published documents and memoirs connected with Louis' *métier* – is in his discovery that, though the formal court life was a necessity and fulfilled certain symbolic and social functions, it had little significance for the exercise of the King's profession and consumed only a very small portion of his working day.

Every Monday, Wednesday and Saturday the ministerial council, the *conseil d'en haut*, met for the whole morning, and continued – if necessary – in the afternoon. At these council meetings where Louis presided he asked for opinions, put pertinent questions, demanded memoranda or elucidations by word of mouth; draft dispatches to royal *intendants* and to French diplomats serving abroad were read and amended; incoming letters were read in full, or in part. Louis also saw ministers and other experts individually, but the work at the *conseil* remained the most significant, enabling the King to obtain differing views and arguments on which to base his own decision. No minutes were kept of these meetings, though Louis' personal secretary made notes for the King's own use; but discussions can frequently be deduced from marginal comments and changes in dispatches. On Tuesdays and Thursdays a council concerned with financial matters, the *conseil d'état*, met in the mornings. Louis took a good deal of interest in its work and attended regularly for the first part of his reign; after that he skipped meetings if he had more urgent matters in hand. Friday mornings were set aside for consultations with the religious leaders of France, the so-called *conseil de conscience*; the Archbishop of Paris usually had audience on that day; the King also spoke at length with his confessor and visiting ecclesiastics were given audience. While Harlay de Champvallon was Archbishop of Paris, from 1671 to 1695, and Père de la Chaise was the royal

88

confessor, these two had the strongest influence on the King in religious matters, but the aged Le Tellier at a particular moment, that of the Revocation of the Edict of Nantes, played what would seem to be a decisive role and Harlay was not consulted.

Outside the regular routine, Louis saw diplomats returning from and going to important missions, commanders of French armies at the end of campaigns or called to Versailles during campaigns for consultations, experts of various kinds, and he gave audience also to foreign diplomats and embassies. Those from Genoa (1685) and from Siam (1687) created the greatest stir; the latter because it came from such a far-away land, the former because it included, at Louis' insistence, the Doge himself, who normally did not leave Genoa. Both occasions were liberally reported in prints and engravings; as were the court entertainments, the great fêtes and celebrations in particular, but also the more ordinary amusements such as the evening 'appartements' with their lotteries, card games and splendid buffets of fruit and sweetmeats.

Reception of the Doge of Genoa. The Dauphin on the left; Louis' brother, Philippe, and his son, young Philippe, on the right. Note the silver furniture and the sunburst decorating the silver throne.

It is surprising that Louis found time for other activities beyond his regular outdoor exercise and his 'relaxation' hobbies connected with the building and landscape gardening programme. But the *métier* of kingship, as well as his growing preoccupation with foreign policy, turned his thoughts to history; a *lecteur* for this subject, de Périgny, was engaged in 1663 and the past, especially the period of the Roman emperors, was studied, while more recent writers, such as Machiavelli, were examined and pondered. Colbert had hitherto done preparatory work for a chronicle of the reign. Louis now began to jot down his thoughts on affairs of state in notes (*feuilles*) which were entered into a book (*registre*) by Périgny, and after his death by Pellisson. The *feuilles* became the basis for the *Mémoires* (covering 1661–68) which Louis dictated, or corrected if Périgny or Pellisson had drafted a chapter: the memoirs would serve, Louis emphasized, both as instructions for his son and as a means of putting the historical record right as to his own motives and guidelines. As a whole they form, as Sonnino has pointed out, an implicit commentary on Machiavelli's *Prince* and *Discourses*, and constitute a major literary effort. After 1672 Louis' *feuilles* concentrate – partly because he was so embroiled in war, but partly also because he had said what he wished to say on politics and society – on his campaigns. They form the so-called *mémoires militaires*, which present strategic problems as Louis saw them. He kept the *feuilles* with his personal papers and seemed in the summer of 1714, when he made his will and generally considered the future, to have contemplated their destruction. Instead he gave them

Le Buffet. Chardin's treatment in paint of a pyramid of fruit.

Opposite, top: A lottery of 1675 in progress at Versailles. Louis XIV used lotteries to provide entertainment and presents in the form of prizes.

Below: A buffet for one of the evening receptions at Versailles, the so-called *'appartements'*. Note the pyramid of fruit.

91

to the Marshal de Noailles, who – after the King's death – placed them in the Royal Library. Historians have therefore been able – but have done so only in recent years – to discover the way in which these *mémoires* were composed.

Other valuable historical material has been lost. All documents collected by Racine and Boileau, Louis' historiographers, were accidentally burnt in a fire at Versailles in January 1716, though some of their historical writings (e.g. Racine's history of the Dutch war) had already been printed.

On his death-bed Louis deliberately arranged for the destruction of the major part of those personal papers which, in several '*cassettes*' to which only he possessed the keys, had survived the clearing-up of 1714. On 28 August he ordered the *cassettes* to be brought in and his room cleared of all attendants. With the help, first of the Chancellor Voysin and Mme de Maintenon and, later, of Mme de Maintenon alone, he then went through the contents. When others were allowed into the room once more, there was evidence of 'much paper having been burnt in the grate'; Mme de Maintenon revealed at a later date that her letters to the King – and his to her – were destroyed that day.

Louis kept quiet (or did not preserve any notes he may have made on the topic) on one of the most puzzling of his actions, the Revocation of the Edict of Nantes in 1685. The revocation is troublesome for several reasons. The Huguenots had been loyal during the *Frondes* and even helped the crown with money; Mazarin had been grateful to them and the King was not likely to forget their services in so critical a period. Furthermore, Louis was by inclination tolerant in religious matters, partly because he himself was not of a religious temperament in the sense of being interested in the subtleties of doctrinal controversy or drawn to mystic religious experiences. For him the main criterion was loyalty to the state and here the Jansenists, with their *frondeur* past, and the Quietists, threatening to undermine the basis of Church and society, seemed much more of a danger than the French Protestants. But Louis was also concerned to avoid controversy that might weaken, even if it did not disrupt, the cohesion of the state in matters of religion. There is a telling comment of his in which he favours the free exercise of the Jewish religion, 'if it can be done without giving offence to the Catholic Church'.

The opposition to the Huguenots came, after the *Frondes*, in the first place from the Church, not from the court. Many churchmen were anxious to bring the French Protestants back to the 'true Church' by missionary work; others were indignant that the Huguenots had taken advantage of the troubled times since 1598 to interpret the Edict of Nantes in such a way that their temples had multiplied outside the enumerated places. Several ministers, and especially the devout Le Tellier, agreed with the complaints of the latter group of churchmen that the Huguenots had become 'a state within the state', and urged curtailment of their present proud freedom. Louis was easily prevailed upon to ensure, by a series of measures enacted from 1669 onwards, that the French Protestants were cut back to their original concessions: in the 1670s temples built after 1598 had to be razed, Protestant burial could take place only at night, and various inducements to conversion were decreed, such as the free distribution of a great many Catholic devotional books and financial rewards for returning to the Church of Rome.

Jean Racine and Nicolas Boileau, distinguished *literati*, whom Louis appointed historiographers royal.

Attack on the Jesuits whose greed is contrasted with 'voluntary poverty'.

But Louis, like some of the Church leaders, hoped initially for papal con-cessions in the matter of the Eucharist which would permit the Huguenots to come back of their own free will; he was against forced conversions and dis-graced the *intendant* who first made use of the *dragonnades* to scare the Huguenots into giving up their faith. His own attitude is evident in his comment at the time of the Siam embassy visit that, just as green leaves of trees differed subtly in colour, God had given man religions of slightly different hues. Pressure from within the French Catholic Church Louis could have withstood, but when to this pressure was added the consciousness that he stood wanting in *gloire* compared with the Emperor and other princes who fought the Turks after 1682, he agreed that the Edict of Nantes should be revoked, though he stipu-lated (in the Edict of Fontainebleau which effected the repeal) that the Hugue-nots were still entitled to liberty of conscience. Three contributory factors can be discerned. Le Tellier, ill and preparing himself for death, urged the King for his own salvation to effect the Revocation; other advisers stressed the glory which would be uniquely his if he succeeded where Henri IV and Louis XIII had failed and ended the religious schism within France; Louis himself believed that his relations with Pope Innocent XI – stormy over such matters as the *régale** and the general determination which the King shared with his As-

LOUIS AND THE REVOCATION
OF THE EDICT OF NANTES

* Louis had extended the crown's right (ceded by the Pope) to income from certain bishoprics, between the death of one incumbent and the appointment of the next, to the whole of France.

LUDOVICO MAGNO

A l'aspect de ce front ou Mars s'est peint luy même,
France, beni l'auteur de ta gloire Supreme,
Que la triste Heresie en palisse d'effroy
Le voici ce Heros qui la force à Se rendre
Qui fait pour ton bonheur tout ce qu'on peut attendre
D'un Pere, d'un Chretien, d'un Conquerant d'un Roy.

Paris chez Haronelman graveur. Rue Jalande proche la place Maubert
tenant la Croix blanche avec Privil. du Roy. 1686.

Celebration of Louis XIV as the 'conqueror of heresy', 1686.

sembly of Clergy to keep the 'Gallican liberties' free from papal interference – might be improved by the Revocation. There is no evidence that his French initiative was meant as a prelude to a Second Counter-Reformation; indeed, Louis accepted and to some extent needed the division of Europe into Catholic and Protestant states.

In his hope of papal approval Louis was disappointed, but in France his action was praised to the skies by Catholics, Jansenists, Jesuits and Gallicans alike. In Protestant countries Louis was condemned; French tolerance in religious matters had been a fact for so long that many Dutch and English Protestants had settled in France in the knowledge that they could freely exercise their own religion. Louis' step seemed a retrograde one and from 1685 he was thought of as a fanatic intent on conversion by the sword. It certainly cost Louis dear in reputation in these countries and contributed to their revulsion against France after 1685. Detrimental effects on French economy were for long held as gospel, mainly for psychological reasons since it satisfied a desire for 'due punishment' to assume that Louis XIV was ruined by the flight of some 10 per cent of the Huguenots (who in all numbered nearly 2 million) abroad in spite of the ban on their leaving the country. Recent research has modified this picture in respect of economic life. It seems certain that the manufacture of clocks and watches suffered a setback for about ten years, and that in some industries, such as papermaking, and in some areas of financial expertise, as also in learning and in the arts and crafts, the host-countries of the refugees benefited. But it is equally clear that in general terms France did not 'suffer' in her economic and financial life from the Huguenot exodus; some of the refugees returned home and others, who remained abroad, either helped France (as did the Huguenot bankers of Geneva) or refrained from taking service with France's enemies, trusting that if they remained 'loyal Frenchmen' God would in time soften Louis XIV's heart and make him grant them free practice of their religion once more. From the point of view of the nineteenth- and twentieth-century respect for individual liberty, Louis' revocation seems abominable; from the Catholic point of view of his own time it ended a blot on French religious honour and united Frenchmen in the true Church. In practical respects the loss was soon made good, if accidentally, by the thousands of Catholic Irish and Scottish Jacobites who fled to France after 1688 and took the places in the ports of the west not only of French Huguenots but also of those English and Dutch non-naturalized subjects who had been ship-chandlers and factors in the wine trade but had returned to their native countries when the repressive measures began.

Religious dissent inside the Catholic Church continued, however, throughout Louis' reign. The King's distrust of Jansenism was a legacy of the *Frondes* and was deepened by his very inability to understand the finer points of Jansenist disputes with the Jesuits. The issues at stake between the orthodox Catholics and the Quietists were easier to grasp, though Louis himself was unable to appreciate Fénelon's glorification of the contemplative religious life; and once more the King's weight was thrown into the scales against those whose doctrines seemed to loosen the moral bonds which the Church provided. Guyonism and Quietism seemed in France – like Molinism in Italy – a dis-

solvent of the very fabric of morality and had to be stamped out. Mme de Maintenon, worried about the spread of 'enthusiasm' in the girls' school at Saint-Cyr
which she and Louis had founded after their marriage, regretted her earlier
friendship with Mme de Guyon – who had in the first place infected the girls
and their teachers, – and helped to discredit the movement. The King's horror
of divisive forces was decisive; even his Gallican attitude *vis-à-vis* the Pope
was modified in his determination to stop Jansenism and Quietism. The bull
Unigenitus, which he asked for and obtained in 1713, made significant concessions (though not of vital importance for the independence of the Gallican
Church) to the Pope in return for a clear condemnation of all anti-orthodox
beliefs.

The work of Louis XIV and his advisers, and the way decisions were
arrived at, remained in part hidden even from the view of contemporaries,
though action revealed what had been decided. The court, on the other hand,
operated in full view, both at the royal and courtier level. At the royal level the
most noticeable feature as Louis got older was his increasing responsibility for
his grown-up family and his having to handle not only the squabbles between
Philippe, his wives and his favourites, but also those between the second and
third generations of his own and his brother's progeny. In addition, after 1688,
there were the exiled Stuarts to take into account. The palace of Saint-Germain-
en-Laye was set aside for their residence with a pension of one million *livres* a
year (which never proved enough) to defray their expenses; but they were also
frequent guests at Versailles, and Louis often had to apply himself to smoothing
relations between their entourage and those in attendance on the various members of his own family.

Louis and his family in 1697. At the
marriage of the duc de Bourgogne
and Marie-Adélaïde of Savoy. The
Dauphin is at Louis' side; Philippe
d'Orléans, to the right, with his
second wife, Liselotte von der Pfalz.

The march of time can be measured by the contrast between Louis and his family depicted in 1669 as gods of the Olympus and any of the paintings or engravings of the extended family in the 1690s. The cherubs and cupids, and infants nearly indistinguishable from them, have been replaced by mortals, dressed in the height of fashion, the ladies usually with patches, and strongly individualized, however flattering the artist's brush or the engraver's pen.

The courtiers formed a race apart, but fulfilled a special and more functional role which historians have only recently begun to dissect, namely that of serving as commission-agents at court, selling at a given percentage their offices as go-betweens with a monarch who was in theory accessible to every subject but who in practice did not have the time to see all who wished to see him or seek his favour. Versailles was wide open, its gates never shut, and the King was known to receive deputations and individuals during his morning passage along the *Grande Galerie* after church service. Anyone decently dressed could go into the park and wander at will to view the gardens, the fountains and the statues (in contrast to the strict security measures taken on hunting expeditions, for fear of accidents or assassination). If visitors desired to see the palace they had to be attired as gentlefolk, which meant, in the man's case, that he had to carry a sword; and swords were discreetly hired to those who did not possess such a symbol of status. But to get close to Louis XIV was virtually impossible for casual visitors since he was protected and guarded by the courtiers. His movements inside the palace were heralded by the cry of 'the King' and by the scurry of those in attendance on him. When he came out of the palace, it put a visiting Italian diplomat in mind of a queen bee surrounded by a swarm of drones leaving the hive. There was therefore a livelihood to be made at court, either in arranging (for payment) opportunities for someone to meet Louis, or – more generally – in taking money for agreeing to bring *placets* or other matters to the King's notice. Louis' mistresses, Louise de La Vallière as well as Athénaïs de Montespan, did so, and indeed, many judged that female courtiers did better in the business than the male ones. Others, and here the males proved most successful, increased their income by skilful card-play; the Marquis de Dangeau virtually supported himself in his early years at court by his unrivalled expertise at the gaming-tables.

The formal life at Versailles, with its 25,000 inhabitants – courtiers, officials and servants – proved wearing at times as Louis XIV got older. In the days of Louise de La Vallière and Athénaïs de Montespan he had been able to relax and get a change of scene in the houses he built for them: the Hôtel de Brion built for Louise in the Palais Royal grounds, the 'porcelain' Trianon for Athénaïs at Versailles. The equivalent in his later years was his transformation of the little 'porcelain' Trianon into the 'Grand Trianon' – in spite of its name a relatively simple building but of the most exquisite marble and coloured stone; and later still of the complex at Marly, where the King's apartments were flanked by a row of buildings for guests. Both palaces had fine gardens, colourful (in contrast to the green and white of Versailles), especially in the tulip-season, as Louis became a willing victim of tulipomania. They were used for

The marquis de Dangeau whose 'journal' – in effect a diary of the King's engagements from 1682 to 1715 – is an important source for Louis XIV's day-to-day life in this period.

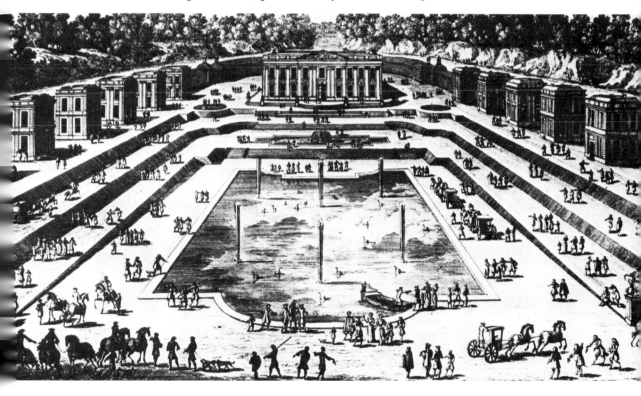

Design for fountain in the grounds of Marly.

Tulipomania. Four million bulbs were imported for Louis yearly from the Dutch Republic in peacetime; in times of war it was considered un-patriotic to send French currency into the pockets of the enemy.

Opposite, above: The richly decor-ated antechamber (*salon de gardes*) of the Queen.

Below: Le Brun's 'month of Feb-ruary'.

relaxation, for evening supper parties and concerts in the case of the Trianon and for what we might describe as weekend visits at Marly; in either case Louis XIV himself chose those who were to be his guests and thus ensured the absence of friction among them.

This need to seek relief from formal court life, at times experienced as oppressive, should not be interpreted as a decline in Louis' attachment to Versailles. Versailles remained the embodiment and the symbol of the monarchy and of his achievement. It had grown with the reign and was not completed till 1710, though its final form, as set in its contrived landscape, had emerged in the 1680s. All French kings had chosen a symbol, an emblem by which they were identified; that of Henri IV had been the salamander, others had chosen porcupines and crescent moons. In Louis' case the symbol so to speak gave itself; the sun, appearing from behind a cloud, had been used by Louis XIII to publicize the birth of his son and this emblem was repeated at Louis XIV's coronation festivities, the ballet costume chosen for him being that of the Sun. The sun is, of course, a symbol beloved of all rulers throughout history, expressing paternalism at its best. It had been utilized by earlier French kings, but was particularly associated with the rulers of the Roman Empire. According to seventeenth-century historical periodization men still lived 'in Roman times',

and at the carousel to celebrate the birth of his son and heir in 1662 Louis chose to be dressed as a Roman emperor.

Increasingly, under the impetus of the classical learning of the members of the *Petite Académie*, the sun was appropriated as Louis' emblem, and the myth of Apollo, the sun-god, was reserved in poetry and in pictorial and plastic decoration for the King. The Apollo theme was consciously woven into the very fabric of Versailles and its grounds. The group, Apollo and the muses, in the Grotto of Thetis, completed in 1668, had to be sacrificed when the rebuilding of the palace had proceeded far enough to demand an enlarged setting; it is known to us only from contemporary engravings. Three other groups of statuary from the 1660s have, however, survived which enable us to grasp the King and his advisers' conception of what the gardens should celebrate. One of these, Apollo in his chariot, presents no problem of interpretation; the visitor today, as in the past, marvels at its perfect placement – low enough not to interrupt the view from the terrace, imposing and commanding when seen close to. But though Apollo does not appear in the other two groups, both use the Apollonian legend in ways more significant to contemporaries than the mere celebration of the sun-god. In the dragon-fountain, Apollo's slaying of the Python symbolizes Louis XIV's destruction of the divisive forces of the *Fronde*: the dragon is pierced by Apollo's arrow, child-figures swim peacefully and safely in the basin. The Latona-fountain was even easier to interpret for those who had lived through the *Fronde*, and it was meant to serve as an object-lesson to those who knew of it only by hearsay: Latona, the mother of Apollo and Diana (hence easy to identify as the Queen-Regent Anne), is protecting her children, and those who had threatened to harm them have, as in Ovid's *Metamorphoses*, been turned into frogs.

The classicism of the age, encouraged by such finds as the antique Venus of Arles in 1651 (which became, so art-historians have deduced, the model for Lantona) and by the preoccupations of artists with Greek and Roman sculpture, was wedded also to realism. The Marsy brothers, who made the Latona group, were realistic enough in their treatment of Ovid's peasants and frogs; so

Louis XIV as 'the Sun' in a ballet of 1665.

The chariot of Apollo built by Tuby.

was Tuby in the horses of his Apollo group. Realistic observance is also characteristic of the decorative sculptures of the park. This is particularly true of the faces and figures of the goddesses, nymphs and children carved by Le Hongre, Coysevox and Girardon, but we note it also in the representations of the rivers of France – the Saône and the Rhône, the Seine and the Marne, the Garonne and the Dordogne – as reclining watergods, surrounded by the symbols of plenty, ears of corn, fruits and children. Louis' own taste certainly combined love of the classical with insistence on realism. The power of Puget, brought to Versailles in 1688 after working in Toulon on ordnance and ships, was especially appreciated by the King, who bought his Milo of Crotona group, now in the Louvre. Even in representations of himself Louis began in middle age to encourage realism: the big ceremonial portrait by Rigaud is true to life even to the tired eyes and the sunken mouth after the 1685 extraction of teeth in the upper jaw; the *embonpoint* of middle age is clearly visible in paintings and prints which show the whole figure. The vanity and self-consciousness of youth had gone. It seemed a long time since 1665 when Louis had been worried at the irregular shape of his nose on first contemplating Bernini's fine portrait bust. On the whole, as he got older Louis was not too pleased at the many commissions for busts and figures on horseback that streamed to Versailles from provincial towns: France was rapidly being disfigured, he protested, with likenesses of himself. Simplicity also replaced fine dress; the preferred garment in later years was a plain brown coat.

Versailles in 1680 before the Latona fountain (centre) was raised.

La Saône by Tuby.

Left: Child by Le Hongre in the fountain of Diana.

Right: *Vénus accroupie*. Sculpture by Coysevox. Note the realism of the flaccid stomach muscles and deformed toes.

Below: Nymph by Le Hongre in the fountain of Diana.

Puget's caryatid for the Hôtel de Ville of Toulon.

Right: Puget's *Milo of Crotona*, the realism of which appealed to Louis, but not to the court in general. It was placed in the royal *allée* at Versailles in 1683, and a companion-piece, the *Perseus and Andromeda*, was ordered and set up in 1685.

The river Garonne. Sculpture by Coysevox.

Portrait of the aging Louis, less well-known than the ceremonial Rigaud painting, but showing the same sunken mouth.

The realism of the older Louis is evident also in other fields than art. Self-deception may be the weakness of absolute rulers and Louis, like all humans, had to work within the boundaries of his own limitations. He was, it is now generally agreed, above rather than below average in intelligence. Though he frequently misjudged situations abroad (in the Netherlands, in the Empire and in England) he learnt from experience and in his maturity grew humble enough to admit that he, like others, could mistake the road to desired goals, especially to that of peace. By 1698 he was wise enough to urge a diplomat sent to Vienna: do not boast of France's strength, that will only bring a new coalition against us; on the other hand, do not make us out so weak as to let others think they can crush us without meeting resistance. The moderation of attitude over the Spanish succession is one that has astonished the last generation of historians who have examined the negotiations which led up to the partition treaties: Louis came to terms with the fact that the Maritime Powers would not partition in such a way that the balance of power in their view became tilted in the favour of France. He agreed to the designation of princes with less Spanish blood than his own grandsons as main heirs to Carlos II (first Joseph Ferdinand and, after his death in 1699, the Archduke Charles of Austria in 1700), accepting the fact that either of his younger grandsons was *persona non grata* to the Dutch and the English: though no union of crowns would follow, it was argued that a union of strategic, economic and colonial interests would. In return Louis was promised territorial advantages which would directly benefit France: it was stipulated that the Dauphin would receive as his share the Spanish-Italian possessions which could, by exchanges, be used to strengthen the eastern frontier. The Spanish western frontier-province of Guipúzcoa would also go to the Dauphin.

Sketch of Louis XIV on horseback by Puget, who had been well received at Versailles in 1688. The projected statue (for Marseilles) was not carried out.

Anti-French cartoon showing Philip V bringing Louis XIV the milk wrung from the Spanish cow. In reality, Spanish ministers wished for a French-born king so that they might benefit from Louis' military power to avoid partition and, also, profit from reforms on the French model in administration and economic life – hopes that were in the main fulfilled.

When Carlos II's will made Philip of Anjou the heir of first choice, Louis hoped against hope that his sacrifice of these territorial gains would mollify the Maritime Powers. His dilemma was a cruel one, for if he did not accept on his grandson's behalf a will which demanded acceptance of the Spanish empire in its entirety, the same offer would be passed on to the heir of second choice named in Carlos' will, the Archduke Charles: it seemed more sensible to sacrifice the territories promised in the partition treaties than to help re-fashion a Habsburg ring round France. Louis' hope that the general peace might be kept, even if Leopold should go to war, was not fulfilled, mainly because the competition for Spanish and Spanish-American trade – which brought gold into the coffers of Europe – had become acute between France and the Maritime Powers.

In the long drawn-out struggle that followed, historians of the present generation have found Louis' most impressive years: his dogged resistance, his compassion for the suffering of his people, his search for peace and his skilful exploitation of the changes in England in 1710 which secured terms favourable to the French position in Europe. Some losses were exacted overseas to the benefit of Britain (Acadia, part of Newfoundland and St Christopher in the West Indies), but these were of lesser importance in view of the French colonial development of the time. Louis had further to promise not to disturb the Protestant Succession and to send James III out of France – both had been a foregone conclusion for years. The only humiliating condition was the destruction of Dunkirk harbour, the privateering port most dangerous to the English. In return France gained Orange – the enclave of William III's patrimony – and, by minor exchanges which made the Barcelonette French, a more easily defensible frontier with Savoy. A more significant gain was English agreement that Philip V should retain the position to which Carlos' will had called him. The danger of a Habsburg encirclement had been conquered and the 'Family

LOUIS AND THE PEACEMAKING OF 1711 TO 1714

The end of the war of 1709

Above: The recruits.
After the bad winter of 1708–09, recruitment became easier. Men flocked to the army to get something to eat.

Centre: Battle of Malplaquet of 11 September 1709 – in which allied losses were large enough to spark off a peace campaign in England which Queen Anne supported.

Publication in Paris of the Anglo-French suspension of arms, 24 August 1712. Note the beginnings of a new style in the pictorial dissemination of news.

The Duke of Berwick, whose victories in Spain had helped convince the English that they would have to accept Philip V.

Proclamation in Paris of the Peace of Utrecht, 1713. The Peace consisted of individual treaties between France and Spain on the one hand and England, Portugal, Savoy and the Dutch Republic on the other.

Compact' of the Bourbons was a fact. Most important, the eastern frontier had been saved; the medal of 1699 with its inscription *Securitas Alsatiae*, remained valid. From the point of view of the verdict of history – as Louis' time conceived its judgments – the King could rest assured that his *gloire* was safe: he had not diminished the realm entrusted to his safekeeping.

LOUIS AND EUROPE
AFTER 1714

Common sense and realism are noticeable also in the politics of the last years of Louis' reign. On the death of Queen Anne of Britain he refused to disturb the Protestant Succession and did not support the 1715 rebellion in Scotland when the Jacobites raised the Stuart standard in favour of James III. Peace with the Emperor and the Empire in 1714 was followed by Louis' overtures for an alliance between Bourbon and Habsburg. Since the Peace of Utrecht had confirmed Philip V's retention of the Spanish throne (though at the implied cost of sacrificing all Spain's Italian possessions), France's southern frontier was safe; cooperation with Vienna seemed the best way to ensure that the gaps in the eastern frontier – where Lorraine still eluded France but where the fortress Landau had been gained to counterbalance Philippsburg – would not be exploited. His offer was examined, but since Turkey's declaration of war on Venice came about the same time, old suspicions raised their heads: was Louis

A turning point in the war, the French army's defeat and flight at Turin in 1706; this led to Louis' abandonment of the Italian front.

ALMANACH ROYAL

Allegorical presentation of the peace-makings between Louis XIV, the Emperor Charles VI and the Empire, published in the *Almanach royal* of 1714, celebrating the Peace of Rastadt of 6 March 1714 and that of Baden, 7 September 1714.

sincere, or was this a trick? The 'Diplomatic Revolution' had to wait till Austria abandoned the 'old system' in 1756, but Louis had seen the logic of the post-1714 situation.

While Louis' attitude to France in relation to Europe underwent a realistic reappraisal in the years 1697–1715, the period also provided a reappraisal in home affairs, though this has been less studied; indeed, the majority of historians have seen the new trends in France as arising only in opposition to Louis XIV. This view will not stand up to examination of archive material which shows that royal initiative, or encouragement of the initiative of others, lies behind the extraordinary activity of these years. The movement away from reliance on income from land is typical of this initiative. The long-standing concern to develop French colonies in the West Indies and French possessions in Nouvelle France and Acadia was given a new dimension in these years. The beaver-trade of the north was no longer profitable – too many pelts had lowered prices – and new plans were formed to adapt to new circumstances. Settlements, linking those on the Great Lakes via the big river-system to the Gulf of Mexico, were made, Louisiana on the Mississippi celebrating Louis' name.

Voyages of discovery were financed by the crown in order to probe whether in the Southern Seas France might be able to find land not effectively occupied by the Portuguese or the Spaniards. Louis realized the need for France to find new sources of wealth. 'The present war', he said of the War of the Spanish Succession, 'is a struggle for the commerce of the Spanish Indies and the riches which they produce.' The findings of the *Conseil de Commerce* of 1700 on how to enhance the standing of the merchant classes were accepted and the older decree that participation in overseas trade would not bring derogation of

LOUIS' SECOND PERIOD
OF REFORM AT HOME

nobility was extended to wholesale trade even inside France. The merchants'
desire to achieve 'automatic' nobility – once they had achieved a certain fortune
or a given number of generations in trade – was not granted, but ennobling for
mercantile services at the king's will now became a significant feature of
Louis' later years when the concept of the *commerce honorable* was put into
practice and the crown and its servants were in the forefront of those who
worked for reform, helping to abolish monopolies, to cut domestic customs-
barriers and get rid of harmful restrictions. From the late 1690s onwards Louis
even attempted, though without success, to have a uniform system of weights
and measures introduced. Here, as elsewhere, the very extent of France and the
strength of provincial and sectional interests worked against innovations and
reforms. The merchants, to give but one example, resisted the participation of
noblemen in domestic trade, judging it unfair competition.

Generally speaking, the verdict on Louis' reign in domestic history is today
more favourable than ever before. French legal historians have concluded, from
their examinations of records, that far from being arbitrary and unjust Louis
showed in various ways respect for the law while the Parlements, 'the nobility
of judges', skilfully used their considerable remaining powers to bolster their
own economic interests and to block by subtle tactics any change regarded as
inimical either to the landowning class (to which they themselves increasingly
belonged) or to the social hierarchical *status quo*. Case histories show peasants
bankrupted, royal taxation reforms opposed and local privileges and traditions
tenaciously defended on the one hand; Louis, on the other, emerges as concerned with justice in the implementation of the law. The *Grands Jours* at the
beginning of the personal reign, once condemned as summary justice, are now
seen as justified punishment of lawless petty nobles. Before levying the *dixième*
Louis in 1710 asked the law faculty of the Sorbonne to determine whether he
had the right, even in wartime, to tax all subjects one-tenth of their fortune.
The tax, highly unpopular with the propertied classes in spite of its certified
legality, had to be relinquished as soon as the desperate war situation eased.
The *paulette*, always resented by office-holders, was also sacrificed in the later
years of the reign. More positively, the codes of Louis XIV – the civil code of
1667, the criminal code of 1670, the maritime code of 1672, the commercial
code of 1673 and the *Code Noir* of 1685 (in respect of the rights of slaves in the
French colonies) – have been found to be in the growing humanitarian tradition so typical of the late seventeenth century. It has also been noted that after
1680 no proceedings against witches were ever brought in France, while the
'poisoning affair' led in 1682 to a law which made registers for the sale of all
poisonous substances compulsory. The infamous royal *lettres de cachet*, which
imprisoned a man, or a woman, by a mere rescript of the King, have on examination been shown as used principally at the request of private individuals
of standing who wished to control their offspring, particularly where property
was involved.

It may well be that the pendulum has swung too far,* but it is worth pointing

* Certainly *lettres de cachet* were also used by Louis XIV for political reasons, e.g. to
imprison Mme de Guyon for eight years for her 'religious enthusiasm' and its
dangerous example.

out that in other fields where archives have been consulted in detail a comparable picture has emerged of paternalistic absolutism striving for rationalization with the help of advisers of like mind. One criticism remains of the King in the legal sphere – that he interfered with fundamental law by having his legitimized sons, the duc de Maine and the comte de Toulouse, put into the French line of succession; but this act can be politically justified. It must be remembered, first, that it took place in 1714 when Louis' great-grandson was the only heir apparent since Philip V, at Anglo-Dutch insistence, had renounced the prospect of the French throne for himself and his sons, and secondly, that the two (contrary to what is sometimes stressed) were put after the princes of the blood – the Orléans and the Condé families – who kept their premier right to succession if young Louis should die without heirs of his own body.

When old Louis was on his death-bed, in August 1715, he was acutely conscious of the fact that he was leaving the country to face a minority with all this implied for France. 'The little one', he said to those advisers he trusted, 'will have a lot to go through; I was a king at five years of age and I well remember the troubled times that came my way.' He felt close to the child – the only legal heir to the throne whom God had spared in the terrible years 1711– 14 – but was concerned also for the illegitimate son he had always loved. While Philippe of Orléans was to be regent for the duration of the minority, his power was hampered by a regency council and the duc de Maine was charged with the supervision of the future king's education and with control of the 'Maison du Roi'.

Louis' mind also surveyed and judged his own reign. Had he been too attracted to war? He thought so, looking back, and in measured and eloquent words advised his great-grandson not to follow his example. The most trustworthy version of the words he spoke to the future Louis XV carry an element of self-defence; *ne m'ymitez pas surtout dans les guerres avec vos voisons, soulagez votre peuple le plus que vous pouvez, jay eue le malheur par les nécessités de l état de ne le pouvoir faire.*

History must find Louis guilty of aggression, at least for the 1667 and 1672 wars, however much the defensive aspect of the two later wars, those of 1689 and 1702, can be stressed. Louis' aggressive acts have, however, been put into better perspective as we have become more willing to admit that other nations, those that fought France, also had aggressive or acquisitive motives, as we are beginning to understand the extent to which fear is a driving force in relations between states and how difficult it is to keep the peace. We now tend to analyze less the 'mistakes' committed by Louis in the years 1700–02 than the dilemma posed by his information that the Dutch Republic and the Spanish Netherlands governor, the Elector Maximilian of Bavaria, had agreed to rob Philip of the Southern Netherlands, and his dispatch of French troops to keep them within the Spanish inheritance. We now appreciate that Louis did not 'arrest' the Dutch troops which, by a Dutch-Spanish convention of 1698, garrisoned certain barrier towns in the Southern Netherlands, but that it was William III, alarmed lest Louis should take such a step, who recalled the troops. Similarly, we are aware that, though complex motives were behind Louis' recognition of

Philippe II of Orléans, designated Regent, did not feel bound by Louis' will and on 2 September, the day after the King's death, assumed full control of the government.

LOUIS AND THE VERDICT
OF HISTORY

James II's son as 'King of England' in September 1701, that recognition came long after William III had decided on war with France – indeed after the Grand Alliance had been signed – though we realize also that Louis under-estimated the valuable ammunition he thus provided for William's anti-French propaganda in England.

The tendency to use the threat of force and even violence in his relations with other states would at first sight seem more characteristic of Louis XIV than of his fellow-rulers, though this may be explained by the fact that France's position was more exposed: Louis had a multiplicity of neighbours who might turn against him and inside France there were enclaves, like the principality of Orange (the patrimony of William III) and the papal possession of Avignon, which could be used by these enemies to further their cause. The well-known examples of Louis' threatening behaviour in the 1660s are found on examination to be part and parcel of the struggle for precedence, insistence on salutes, and maintenance of privileges obtained, inseparable from the diplomacy of the period. Though Louis' methods were at times crude and insensitive, he was

The bombardment of Genoa, 24 May 1684. The exactness of the drawing of the ships employed and the explanation of the tactics make this a document of historical importance.

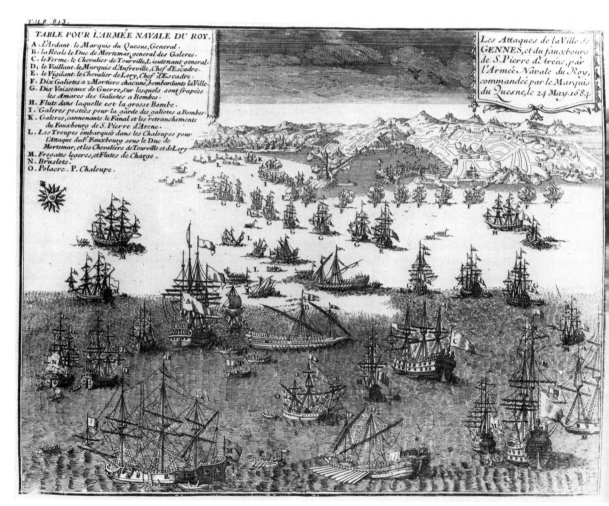

BOMBARDEERT &... ENT BRANDEN T BRUSSELEN. A 169.

on the whole more flexible in his diplomacy and more willing than his fellow-monarchs to find expedients. Louis' acts of violence in the 1680s are, however, blatant. Some historians have judged these so 'untypical' of the King that they have seen him in this decade as confused and dominated by aggressive ministers, such as Croissy and Louvois.

In 1684 Genoa was bombed and three-quarters of its houses laid in ashes; in 1686 Victor Amadeus was bullied into persecuting the Waldensian Protestants (of the Vaud); in 1688 the towns of the Palatinate were ravaged. There are rational explanations for these acts. Genoa was the ally of Spain and continued, after being requested to desist, in giving shelter to and fitting out Spanish galleys which preyed on French shipping in the Mediterranean during the war of 1683–84. The Waldensians commanded a *porte d'entrée* into France and were in their religious zeal willing to serve as a base for Louis' enemies. The burning of the towns of the Palatinate which caused Liselotte von der Pfalz such grief – especially for Heidelberg – was meant to delay invasion by Imperial troops at a time when French fortifications were not yet complete and Louis had few troops in readiness for defence. But Louis himself must take the responsibility for these acts, not his ministers. It may be true that he lost his temper with Louvois and went for him with a pair of fire tongs over an unauthorized threat to burn Trier, but we have only Saint-Simon's word (which is not always to be trusted) for this, whereas in the archives of war there is a great deal of evidence that Louis himself pressed for the destruction of the Palatinate so as to rob his enemies of sustenance and supplies, while offering the population of towns and villages refuge in the Alsace.

It will be noted that the acts of violence cited for 1684, 1686 and 1688–89 were of a character that could come within the definition of 'protective terror' used in the warfare of the period by all commanders when necessity drove them: Marlborough laid the whole of Bavaria waste in 1704, Tsar Peter applied scorched-earth tactics in Poland-Lithuania in 1707–08, Charles XII of Sweden created a zone of safety round his winter-camp in the Ukraine in 1708–09 by evacuating and burning villages. Louis' regrets were, therefore, not for the way he had fought wars, but for the effect of the wars on the French people, bringing hardships which increased those which the vicissitudes of nature – such as the incredibly hard winter of 1708–09 – had inflicted on the poorest sections of society. It may be that, as Louis weakened, the problems of foreign policy which had appeared (and had been) so urgent, receded in im-

The bombardment of Brussels, 1695. Louis' answer to repeated allied attacks on French towns along the Channel coast; he had in vain sought an agreement to refrain from the bombardment and ravaging of centres of civilian population.

113

Felicitas Publica: Allegorical presentation of Louis XIV as the father of the nation.

Opposite, above: The issue of free bread, baked in the Louvre, during a famine period, 1662.

Left: Satire on well-to-do women who resented edicts which limited luxury spending in time of war. Right: Satire on grain merchants who waxed rich during the bad harvests: France has abundance if only the anti-social speculators can be made to disgorge their ill-gotten gains.

portance; but it seems more likely that he was conscious of having, by his aggressions in 1667 and 1672, misinterpreted the 'true interests' of France, thus drawing a nemesis upon himself and the state by his early *hubris*.

Louis knew himself to be innocent of the charge, current in contemporary propaganda (and still accepted by many historians), that he had aimed at 'universal monarchy' by plotting his own election as Emperor of the Holy Roman Empire. Mazarin had indeed put out feelers in 1657 towards the League of the Rhine to see whether he might propose the nineteen-year-old Louis' name in competition with Leopold of Austria, but had been decisively rebuffed. The suggestion that Louis might stand for Imperial election did crop up in the personal reign, being advanced by Brandenburg at one moment of diplomatic negotiations and by Bavaria at another; but there was no substance in the discussions that followed, since Louis was well aware of their unrealistic character. For contemporaries, however, 'universal monarchy' had a wider and vaguer meaning, indicating fear of France's becoming an exorbitant, power-exerting, undue influence in territorial and trade issues – by the very size of its armies and navies and the ambitions of Louis XIV. This fear was, as we have seen, a determining factor especially in the relationship between Louis XIV and the Maritime Powers; though from Louis' point of view the growth in power and riches of the states ruled by William III and by Leopold I was equally destructive of the European balance.

In domestic affairs Louis' conscience was clearer as the issues had been for him less complex. He had always believed, somewhat mechanistically, that men tended to pursue private and selfish interests unless restrained by a just ruler concerned with the safety and prosperity of all subjects. A paternalistic ruler, aware of his duties as head of the body of the state could, he held, fulfil them just because he was the head and could view the rivalries and struggles of the body politic impartially. He knew himself to have been sincere in his efforts to reconcile the nation; the *Frondes* had been suppressed without revenge (Marseilles, for instance, had kept its privileges in spite of its revolt) and Louis had gone out of his way apropros the *Frondes* to stress in his instructions for the Dauphin that every corporate body endowed with power had, throughout history, committed errors and taken the wrong road to solution of problems. He warned his grandson Philip V, when he lent him French troops in 1714 to break the resistance of Barcelona, against massacre of the rebels: the purpose of the siege must be to bring Catalonia into a unified Spain, not to alienate the province by senseless cruelty.

Louis frequently expressed his wish that poverty might be eradicated in France, but whether he thought this achievable in the light of his experience of opposition from the propertied sections of society is not known. Government-inspired propaganda, particularly in broadsheets and cartoons, tried to ridicule and shame profiteers of all kinds, and active steps, such as selling cheap bread direct to the poor, were undertaken to mitigate hardship. There were indeed far fewer riots and risings in his reign than in the first half of the seventeenth century, but some did occur – triggered off by the pressure of taxation or by opposition to the central authority in provinces which had long been used to taking the interest of their own area alone into account. The most serious un-

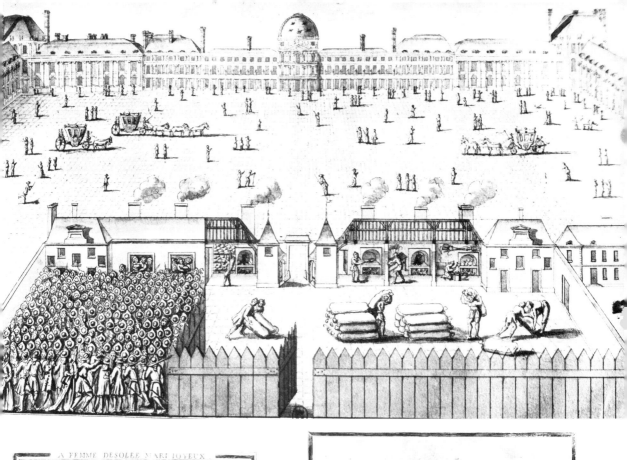

rest, the Protestant rising in the Cévennes during the War of the Spanish Succession, from 1702 to 1704, was, however, religiously motivated. By the end of
the war, when the allied attempt to take Toulon had been defeated and there
was no longer any need to fear Huguenot cooperation with France's enemies,
religious tolerance for Protestants returned in practice if not in theory, both for
the Cévenols and for Huguenots in general.

LOUIS' BELIEFS   Optimism, based on reasoned deductions, was, however, part of the climate
of opinion in which Louis lived and worked, and he may well have been more
hopeful of remedying the lot of the poorer classes of society than seems to us
reasonable. The fundamental dependence of the absolute monarchy on the
propertied classes (or, conversely, the dynastic state run as personal property), so
clear to us, was not so obvious to a ruler who thought of himself as above
sectional interests and was served by like-minded ministers. When Bernini in
1665 called Louis a *roi d'aujourd'hui*, the Italian had in mind his royal patronage
of the arts, but there is a sense in which Louis XIV – even when old and
failing – was in tune with the reforming rationalist spirit of a group of men all
over Europe who were ahead of the times. This elite has, since the mid-
eighteenth century, been widened to include ever larger sections of society
(though the pace has differed in different parts of Europe), so that 'reform from
above' has become redundant. It is, for this reason, difficult for modern Euro-
peans to judge the seventeenth-century would-be reformers fairly or 'non-
politically' without proper historical study. Without historical thinking it is
not easy to interpret words we still use, such as 'order' and 'duty', in the sense
which they had in the seventeenth century. Order as opposed to anarchy was a
seventeenth- and eighteenth-century ideal; order and understanding were conceived of as beauty in society as in art; performance of 'duty' equalled 'utility'
and served the 'true interests' of the state. These ideas Louis shared. He held
that God worked through human agents and he was not overfond of attributing
things to Providence, though Mme de Maintenon had considerable success in
convincing him, on the personal level, that the evils of war and the row of
deaths in his family in 1711–12 were a punishment by God intended to teach
him humility and thus ensure his salvation. On his death-bed he told the duc
d'Orléans that he owed her a great deal, 'especially in the matter of my
salvation'.

LOUIS' HEALTH   Louis' health had been surprisingly good if we think of the voluminous
medical notes which listed every twinge and ache as well as the illnesses: the
measles he caught from the Queen in 1683, the dislocated elbow of 1684, the
operation in 1685 to remove the teeth of the upper jaw to get rid of a troublesome abscess (but which accidentally removed part of the jawbone) and the
successful operation in 1686 for an anal fistula. His digestion troubled him at
times (though the common stories, oft repeated, that his intestines were ab-
normally long and that he had a worm of astounding proportion, are both
erroneous), but the famous purges were nothing more sinister than herbal tea
and rhubarb. His appetite was, as noted above, large (particularly for food
flavoured with herbs, for game and for dishes in which pistachio nuts formed
an ingredient); but on the whole he ate sensibly from the modern point of view;
plenty of vegetables (especially globe artichokes and fresh peas) and fruit grown

at Versailles. Until he was twenty he could not be persuaded to drink anything stronger than fruit juices and water; from then on he drank wine, usually watered. Between 1672 and 1696 Louis drank the champagne recommended by his premier physician, d'Aquin, who held the King to be liverish in constitution; after 1696 d'Aquin's successor, Guy-Crescent Fagon, prescribed burgundy since Louis, in his opinion, was lymphatic and anaemic. Both may have been right in their diagnoses; the bloodletting which was such a feature of medical practice of the age may have weakened Louis. In his last years the King, it would seem instinctively, refused this all-purpose remedy and was in general against 'remedies'.

There were certainly no signs of weakness even as the King entered his seventies. He remained virile; Mme de Maintenon asked her confessor whether it was still her duty to submit to more than one *bonne bouche* (her euphemism for sexual intercourse) a night and was answered in the affirmative. He slept 'like a child'. He continued to hunt from his wagonette and stopped a team of runaway horses when he was seventy-five. He enjoyed concerts and parties at Marly during the first week of August 1715, took part in a stag-hunt and arranged for the court (and himself) to go hunting at Fontainebleau at the end of the month. But on the 10th of August he suddenly felt very ill and moved to Versailles. He was in constant pain, which he tried at first to forget by working with councils, ministers and officials in his room, by calling for music and song, by visits to members of his family in rooms outside his own, by talking to d'Antin (Montespan's son by her husband) – the new *Surintendant des Bâtiments* – about repairs and improvements to buildings, and by encouraging everyone to carry on as normal. Go hunting, he told his sons, *ne perdez point le temps qui est très beau.*

His high fever, his unquenchable thirst and his altered features, however, told those close to him, even before the senile gangrene of his left leg was discovered, that this was the end. Soon he became too weak to leave his bed, except for short periods, and he had to be carried to the chapel when, on the 20th, he wished to attend a service in his father's memory and for the *Fête de Saint-Louis* on the 25th. From the 24th he prepared for death systematically, cancelling the Fontainebleau visit, giving orders that Vincennes should be prepared for the great-grandson who would become Louis XV, having his private papers burnt, seeing ministers and saying farewell to his household and to his family.

He had confidence in the future. 'I depart, France remains', are words noted down from his death-bed. There was a new generation of administrators, trained by himself, who had ideas for continuing reform based on the *enquêtes* in depth of the 1690s and early 1700s, and on memoranda submitted to the King by individual initiative, best known among them Boisguilbert's *critique* of the economy and Vauban's suggested remedies for domestic ills and encouragement of overseas development.

By his will of 1714 Louis had taken care to include the chief ministers (the Chancellor and minister for the army Voysin, Desmaretz, in charge of finance, Pontchartrain for the navy and colonies, and the able Torcy in foreign affairs) in the regency council, as well as four marshals of France who had considerable

The end of life, anonymous painting entitled *Vanity*.

Statue of winter at Versailles, by Girardon.

experience in diplomacy (Villeroi who knew the Germanies well and had negotiated the peacemakings of 1714, Tallard with excellent knowledge of England, d'Huxelles who had negotiated in the Netherlands, and d'Harcourt, an expert on Spain). These men were meant to guide the regent and the other princes of the blood, the duc de Maine and the comte de Toulouse, and the duc de Condé when he had reached the age of twenty-four. Louis had at times been critical of the prospective regent, Philippe d'Orléans, as of the rest of the young fashionable set, with their immoral, Paris-centred life, bent on pleasure (the generation-gap is experienced afresh throughout history), but he had a basic trust that Philippe would grow with responsibility – he had, after all, proved sensible and courageous in the war years during his command in Spain. In any case Louis trusted to the restraints of the regency council where decisions would be by majority, and to the fact that the duc de Maine had been given charge of the Maison du Roi and thus virtually of the army.

Though resigned to death, Louis naturally felt some emotion when saying his farewells. He cried when begging Mme de Maintenon's forgiveness for not having made her happy and when he saw his great-grandson for the last time. The boy's governess, Mme de Ventadour (who by a codicil to the will of April 1715* had been given specific charge of the future Louis XV till he reached an age when Villeroi, his governor, and Maine, the superintendent of his education, should take over), put him into the old King's arms to receive his advice and blessing and felt obliged to remove him when Louis XIV was overcome at the end by a flood of tears. With the rest it was easier; Louis interrupted his farewells to the courtiers and servants of his household when he noticed that they, and he, were being 'afflicted by emotion'.

He was less moved when giving his final blessing to the princes and princesses of the blood. He spoke too low to be overheard in his individual leave-taking, but he raised his voice in a general exhortation that after his death they might live in peace and a *grande union* among themselves; to ministers and other officials whom he saw individually he asked continued faithful service and honest advice in the new reign. The one exception would seem to be with his religious advisers, where a note of self-justification crept in, just as when he touched upon war and peace. He thanked them – including the Cardinal Rohan and his confessor, Père le Tellier – for their care of his soul, but stressed that they would have to answer before God for the advice they had given him 'in recent years'; he himself had in religious matters always had *très bonnes intentions*.

In the last weeks of his life he began to speak of his kingship in the past tense – *Du temps que j étais roi* – and implied that his own life had outlasted his endurance when, on waking, he found Mme de Maintenon in tears by his bedside: 'Did you then think me immortal?'

Whether Louis' will and dispositions in general would be respected he could not know,† but he had done his best. The task of the conscientious ruler

* A second codicil of 23/8 1715 made Fleury preceptor of the future Louis XV.
† The will was indeed upset by the duc d'Orléans, who became sole regent on 2 September 1715. By 1718 the duc de Maine and the comte de Toulouse were deprived of all honours and positions, no longer entitled to being 'Princes of the Blood'.

born to absolutism was not easy. A minister who served an absolutist ruler had some choice whether he wished to accept office or not; so did politicians and statesmen in the oligarchies of the period; even William III chose to exercise the right he felt he possessed in respect of the crown of England. Louis, like other hereditary rulers of his time, had no choice except in so far that they all had the right of abdication. Queen Christina of Sweden had abdicated in 1654 and James II was deemed to have taken this step in 1688 by his flight from England. Louis never contemplated abdication, nor did he, like William III, threaten to abdicate, a threat he would have regarded as incompatible with both *gloire* and duty. While he lived he could not visualize life without the burden as well as the pleasures of kingship. When his time had come to depart life, on Sunday, 1 September 1715, he was ready to go. 'Everyone says it is difficult to die...I find it easy.'

Gates with sun emblem at Versailles.

1638 September 5. Birth of Louis, Dauphin of France.

1640 September 6. Birth of Louis' brother Philippe.

1643 April 21. Ceremonial baptism of Louis.

1643 May 14. Death of Louis XIII, the Dauphin's accession as Louis XIV.

1648–52 Civil war (the *Frondes*).

1651 September 7. Louis declared of age.

1654 June 7. Louis crowned and consecrated as king at Rheims.

1654 (onwards) Louis takes part in campaigns on the northern and eastern frontiers of France.

1658, 1659, 1660 Royal progresses to south and south-west of France.

1660 June 9. Marriage of Louis and Maria Teresa.

1661 March 9. Death of Mazarin, Louis rules henceforth without a *premier ministre*; cabinet and *conseil* government with increasing bureaucratization develops.

1661 July. Louise de La Vallière becomes Louis' mistress.

1661 November 1. Birth of Louis, Dauphin (Grand Dauphin) of France; between 1662 and 1672 five more children were born of marriage to Maria Teresa (two sons and three daughters), none of whom survived infancy and/or childhood.

1662 November 18. Birth of first illegitimate child; between 1663 and 1678 ten more illegitimate children were born and all who survived infancy and early childhood were legitimized.

1663 Device *Nec Pluribus Impar* adopted.

1663–71 Academies founded or reorganized: of Inscriptions and Medals, of Painting and Sculpture, of Science, of Rome, of Music, of Dancing, and of Architecture.

1664 and **1666** *Grands Fêtes* at Versailles (*Plaisirs de l'Ile Enchantée* and *Fête de l'Amour et de Bacchus*).

1665 *Conseil de justice* created to formulate and edit French codes (completed by 1685).

1667 Work begins on Louis' *Mémoires*.
Françoise (Athénaïs) de Montespan replaces La Vallière as Louis' mistress.

1667 (onwards) Versailles: rebuilding and relandscaping.

1667–68 War of Devolution.

1672–78/9 Dutch war.

1673 Louis begins to wear a wig.

1680 City of Paris bestows title *Le Grand* on Louis.

1682 Birth of Louis' first grandchild, a boy. In all, three legitimate grandsons were born alive or survived infancy in Louis' lifetime: from the legitimized children he received nine grandchildren: two grandsons and a granddaughter via the duc du Maine; one grandson and five granddaughters via Françoise-Marie, wife of Philippe II d'Orléans.

1683 Death of Louis' wife Maria Teresa.

1684 Probable date of Louis' second, morganatic marriage to Mme de Maintenon.

1685 Extraction of teeth in upper jaw; complications followed.

1686 Successful operation for an anal fistula.
School of St. Cyr (Hôtel royal de St. Cyr) founded by Louis and Mme de Maintenon.

1688/9–97 Nine Years War.

1694 Louis buys Hôtel Vendôme for academies and archives.

1698 and **1700** Partition Treaties: attempt to solve Spanish succession issue without recourse to war.

1699 *Conseil de commerce* revived, *enquête* into methods to encourage trade; great efforts in respect of overseas trade and exploration.

1700 November 9. Louis accepts the will of Carlos II: his grandson Philippe, duc d'Anjou, proclaimed King of Spain, November 24.

1701 Death of Louis' brother Philippe.

1702–13 War of the Spanish Succession.

1707 First great-grandchildren to survive birth and infancy: Louis, duc de Bretagne, son of the duc de Bourgogne, and Luis, son of Philip V of Spain; each had another son (Louis, duc d'Anjou, b. 1710, and Ferdinand, b. 1713, respectively), making four in all.

1712 *Académie Politique* founded to train foreign-office personnel and diplomats.
Death of Louis' eldest grandson, the duc de Bourgogne, and also of the latter's wife and elder son, the duc de Bretagne.

1714 Death of Louis' youngest grandson, the duc de Berri.
Louis makes his two surviving legitimized sons princes of the blood, capable of succeeding in case the Orléans family and the Condé family should die out in the male line.

1715 August. Louis' illness and final arrangements for the education of his heir, the five-year-old 'little Louis', Dauphin since 1712.

1715 September 1. Death of Louis.

SELECT BIBLIOGRAPHY

I LOUIS XIV'S OWN WRITINGS
Collected writings
The most complete collection, including some texts which have since disappeared, is that edited by Ph. A. Grouvelle, *Œuvres de Louis XIV* (6 vols., Paris 1806). The much-used selection by C. Dreyss, *Mémoires de Louis XIV* (2 vols., Paris 1860), is distrusted by scholars. The recent editions by J. Longnon, *Mémoires pour les années 1661 et 1666* (Paris 1923) and *Mémoires de Louis XIV* (Paris 1928), are good but should be read in conjunction with Paul Sonnino's article, 'The Dating and Authorship of Louis XIV's *Mémoires*', in *French Historical Studies* 1964. Paul Sonnino has translated Louis' *Mémoires for the Instruction of the Dauphin* (New York and London 1970) with an excellent introduction.

Occasional writings
Manière de montrer les jardins de Versailles, ed. R. Girardet (Paris 1951); *Rapports sur l'administration des Bâtiments annotées par le Roi* in *Le Duc d'Antin et Louis XIV*, ed. J.J. Guiffrey (Paris 1869); 'Dialogues entre Louis XIV et Colbert', ed. E. Lavisse in *Revue de Paris* 1900 and 1901.

Letters
These are scattered in *Lettres de Louis XIV au Comte de Briord 1700 and 1701* (Hague 1728); *Lettres de Louis XIV aux princes de l'Europe*, etc. (2 vols., Paris 1755); *Lettres de Louis XIV à Madame la Marquise de Maintenon* (Paris 1822); *Lettres inédites 1693–1711* (from Dépôt de la Guerre, Paris 1828); *Letters of William III and of Louis XIV and of Their Ministers 1697–1700*, ed. P. Grimblot (2 vols., London 1848); *Correspondance de Louis XIV avec M. Amelot, 1705–1709*, ed Baron de Girardot (Nancy 1864); *Quelques Lettres de Louis XIV* etc. *1688–1713*, ed. A. Hiver de Beauvoir (Paris 1862); *Correspondance de Louis XIV et du Duc d'Orléans 1707*, ed. M.C. Pallu de Lessert (Paris 1903). Of the important letters to his grandson Philip V of Spain (see text, p. 114) some are found in *Œuvres*, vols. V and VI, and many more in A. Baudrillart, *Philippe V et la Cour de France* (5 vols., Paris 1890–1900), but not all are yet in print.

II BIBLIOGRAPHICAL HELP
The most exhaustive guides to published documents for the reign, to the memoirs and pamphlet literature and to the classic histories of the reign are E. Bourgeois and L. André, *Les Sources de l'Histoire de France*, vols. III and IV: *XVIIe Siécle 1610–1715* (Paris 1926–28), and S. Honoré, *Catalogue général des livres imprimés de la Bibliothèque Nationale. Actes Royaux*, vols. III and IV: *Louis XIV* (Paris 1946–50). Brief but useful orientations are found in John B. Wolf, 'The Reign of Louis XIV: A Selected Bibliography of Writings since the War of 1914–18', *Journal of Modern History* 1964; John C. Rule, 'The Old Régime in America: A Review of Recent Interpretations of France in America', *William and Mary Quarterly* 1962 and the same author's 'Louis XIV: A Bibliographical Introduction' in the volume of essays *Louis XIV and the Craft of Kingship* noted under III below. The annual list of books in *French Historical Studies* is recommended. For bibliographical help in a wider setting I refer to my *Europe in the Age of Louis XIV* (London 1969) and to R. Pillorget's section in *Guide de l'Etudiant en Histoire Moderne et Contemporaine* (Paris 1971).

III CONTRIBUTIONS IN RECENT SYMPOSIUMS
Historical Essays 1600–1750, ed. H.E. Bell and R.L. Ollard (London 1963): the contribution by John Bromley on privateering.
The Responsibility of Power, ed. Leonard Krieger and Fritz Stern (New York 1967): the contribution by A. Lossky on Louis XIV's political ideas.
La France au temps de Louis XIV, ed. Jacques Goimard (Paris 1967): contributions by Georges Mongrédien, Jean Meuvret, Roland Mousnier, Roger-Armand Weigert, Robert Mandrou, Antoine Adam and Victor-L. Tapié.
William III and Louis XIV, ed. Ragnhild Hatton and J.S. Bromley (Liverpool and Toronto 1968): the contributions by Mark A. Thomson, John C. Rule and Ragnhild Hatton.
Louis XIV and the Craft of Kingship, ed. John C. Rule (Ohio State University Press 1969): contributions by John C. Rule, John B. Wolf, C.D. O'Malley, Ragnhild Hatton, A. Lloyd Moote, H.C. Judge, O. Ranum, N.T. Whitman, H.H. Rowen, A. Lossky, P. Sonnino and W.C. Church.
Studies in Diplomatic History, ed. Ragnhild Hatton and M.S. Anderson (London 1970): the contributions by M.S. Anderson and John C. Rule.
Le Conseil du roi, R. Mousnier et al. (Paris 1970): the contributions by R. Mousnier, J. Bérénger and W. Roth.

IV RECENT MONOGRAPHIC STUDIES OF OUTSTANDING IMPORTANCE
E. Asher, *The Resistance to the Maritime Classes* (University of California Press 1960).
M. Bloch, *Les Rois thaumaturges* (2nd ed. Paris 1961).
F. Bluche, *Les Magistrates du Parlement de Paris* (Paris 1960).
A. Corvisier, *L'armée française de la fin du XVIIe siècle*, vol. I (Paris 1964).
G. Durand, *Etats et Institution: XVIIe Siècle* (Paris 1969).
P. Durye, *L'Annoblissement par charge avant 1789* (Paris 1962).
P. Goubert, *Louis XIV et vingt millions de Français* (Paris 1966). English translation of 1970 to be read with review article 'Translated History', *European Studies Review* 1971.
G. Guitton, *Le Père de la Chaise, confesseur de Louis XIV* (2 vols., Paris 1959).
L. Hautecoeur, *Les Jardins des Dieux et des Hommes* (Paris 1955).
H. Kamen, *The War of the Succession in Spain 1700–1715* (London 1969).
J. Levron, *Châteaux et Parcs Royaux* (Paris 1964, with English translation 1965).
H. Lüthy, *La Banque Protestante en France de la Révocation de l'édit de Nantes*, vol. I (Paris 1959).
H. de Mahuet, *La Cour souveraine de Lorraine et Barrois 1641–1790* (Nancy 1959).
R. Mandrou, *La France au XVIIe et XVIIIe Siècles* (Paris 1967).
H.-J. Martin, *Livre, Pouvoirs et Société à Paris au XVIIe siècle* (2 vols., Geneva 1969).

R. Mousnier, *La Plume, la faucille et le marteau* (reprinted articles, Paris 1970).

F. Olivier-Martin, *Histoire du droit français des origines à la Révolution* (Paris 1948).

J. Orcibal, *Louis XIV et les Protestants* (Paris 1951).

A. Rébelliau, *Vauban* (Paris 1962).

L. Rothkrug, *Opposition to Louis XIV* (Princeton 1965).

H.H. Rowen, *The Ambassador prepares for war: the Dutch Embassy of Arnauld de Pomponne* (Hague 1957).

J. Saint-Germain, *La Reynie et la Police au grand siècle* (Paris 1962).

W.C. Scoville, *The Persecution of the Huguenots and French Economic Development, 1680–1720* (Berkeley and Los Angeles 1960).

J. Shennan, *The Parlement of Paris* (London 1968).

B. Teyssèdre, *L'Art au siècle de Louis XIV* (Paris 1967).

E. Vaillé, *Le cabinet noir* (Paris 1950).

B. Verlet, *Versailles* (Paris 1961).

F. Vidron, *La Vénerie royale au XVIIe siècle* (Paris 1953).

V FRENCH NEW SERIES

An important illustrated series with good bibliographies, 'Univers de la France', published by Edouard Privat, started in 1967. Each volume is devoted to one French province and consists of sizeable contributions (in chronological sequence) by different specialists. All sections for the reign of Louis XIV can be recommended: Languedoc (1967), Provence (1969), Bretagne (1969), Normandy (1970) and Alsace (1970).

VI RECENT ARTICLES IN PERIODICALS OF OUTSTANDING IMPORTANCE
French
Annales, Economies, Sociétés, Civilisations 1952, M. Giraud, 'Crise de conscience et d'autorité à la fin du règne de Louis XIV'.

XVIIe Siècle. Every volume is valuable, but note especially 1955 devoted to French attitudes to various aspects of government; 1959, to Louis XIV's servants; 1960, to Louis XIV's foreign policy; 1966, to economic and financial history.

Historia 1953, L. Madelin, 'Comment le Roi Soleil dirigeait ses Ministres'.

Revue d'Histoire diplomatique 1965, devoted to Louis XIV's foreign policy.

Revue de l'Histoire de Versailles 1937, A. Joly, 'Le Roi-Soleil, histoire d'une image'.

English and American
American Historical Review 1963, R. Forster, 'The Provincial Noble: a reappraisal'.

Economic History Review 1960, R.B. Grassby, 'Social Status and commercial enterprise under Louis XIV'.

French Historical Studies 1962, A. Lloyd Moote, 'The Parliamentary Fronde and Seventeenth Century Robe Solidarity'; 1964, L. Bernard, 'French society and popular uprisings under Louis XIV'.

Journal of Economic History 1962, W. Scoville, 'The French Economy in 1700–1701'.

Past and Present 1967, J.H.M. Salmon, 'Venality of Office and Popular Sedition in Seventeenth Century France'.

NOTES TO THE PICTURES
Dates of artists are given only where they do not appear in the index

Frontispiece. Bust of Louis XIV in Roman dress, 1681, by Coysevox, more than life-size. Musée de Versailles. Photo: Giraudon
Page
6 Henri IV and Marie de Médicis with the infant Louis XIII. Medal *c.* 1603 by Guillaume Dupré (1574–1647). B.N., Paris. Photo: Giraudon

10 *L'Allégresse de la France représentée par des Enfans qui dansent.* B.N., Paris
La Sage femme présentant au Roy Monseigneur le Dauphin. Engraving, 1638, by Abraham Bosse (1602–76). B.N., Paris. Photo: Giraudon

11 Medal by J. Varin, *c.* 1643, showing Louis XIV and his mother, Anne of Austria. B.N., Paris. Photo: Giraudon

13 Louis and his brother Philippe. Detail from an anonymous painting, *Madame Lansac et les Enfants de France.* Musée de Versailles. Photo: Giraudon

14 *Louis XIII couronné par la Victoire.* Painting by Ph. de Champaigne. (b.1602). Louvre. Photo: Giraudon

16 Frontispiece to *Le Cid. Tragi-comédie* by Corneille. (First ed. 1636.) B.N., Paris. Photo: Viollet

17 Anonymous engraving showing the 'Machine de Marly'. Photo: Giraudon

18 *Le Cardinal Prend Soin de l'Education du Dauphin.* Anonymous engraving. B.N., Paris. Photo: Viollet

20 *Les Justes devoirs rendus au Roi et à la Reine Régente.* Anonymous engraving. B.N., Paris. Photo: Viollet
Louis XIV Dans Sa Minorité, portrait (*c.* 1650) by Nicolas Mignard. Château Champs. Photo: Giraudon
Louis XIV, Vainqueur de la Fronde. Anonymous allegorical painting. Musée de Versailles. Photo: Giraudon

21 *Réjouissance Générale des François touchant la Paix.* Anonymous engraving. B.N., Paris.

23 *Le Grand Condé.* Bust, 1678, by Coysevox. Musée Condé, Chantilly

25 *L'Auguste et Royalle Scéance de sa maiesté.* 22 October 1652. Contemporary engraving. Photo: Viollet

26 *Sacre de Louis XIV à Reims*, 7 June 1654. Contemporary engraving. Photo: Viollet

28 *Flotte anglaise et hollandaise devant le port de Dunkerque*, 21 September 1694. Anonymous engraving. B.N., Paris. Photo: Viollet

29 Anonymous portrait of Anne Martinot, princesse de Conti. Musée de Versailles. Photo: Giraudon

30 *Louis XIV ordonnant l'exécution de l'Hôtel royal des Invalides en la plaine de Grenelle*, 1672. Engraving by R. Bonnart (1652–1729). Photo: Viollet

31 Gold medal, 1665, by J. Varin,

celebrating Louis' decision to re-build the Louvre. Photo: Giraudon

Le Quai au Charbon à Paris. Anonymous gouache. Musée des Beaux-Arts, Rheims. Photo: Giraudon

32 *La Pompe de la Samaritaine.* Anonymous engraving. B.N., Paris

32/33 View of Paris from the Pont Neuf towards Pont Royal. Engraving by Jacques Rigaud (c. 1681-1754). B.N., Paris. Photo: Giraudon

32 *Veue et Perspective du Collège des Quatre Nations.* Engraving by A. Pérelle (1638-95). B.N., Paris

33 Machine for erecting an equestrian statue of Louis XIV in Lyons, 27-28 December 1713. Engraving by Sebastian Leclerc (1637-1714). B.N., Paris

The bronze equestrian statue of Louis XIV by Girardon erected in Place Louis le Grand (now Vendôme) in Paris, 13 August 1699. Anonymous engraving. B.N., Paris

Feste publique, Feu d'Artifice et Combat pour Loye entre les Mariniers le 13. Aoust 1699. Anonymous engraving. B.N., Paris

34 *Veüe du Chasteau, des Jardins, et de la Ville de Versailles du costé l'Estang.* Etching, 1674, by Israël Silvestre (1621-91). B.N., Paris

35 Part of the park laid out by Le Nôtre at Versailles. Photo: Giraudon

36/37 *Veüe générale de la Ville et du Chasteau de Versailles du costé des Jardins.* Engraving by Pierre Aveline-le-vieux (1654-1722)

Part of *Manière de faire visiter les Jardins de Versailles,* in Louis' own hand, 1699. B.N., Paris

38 Sketch, 1658, by Charles Le Brun. Private collection. Photo: courtesy Sothebys, London

39 Anonymous portrait of three of the Mancini sisters. Musée du Petit Palaise, Paris. Durvil Collection. Photo: Giraudon

40 Map showing France's vulnerable northern and eastern frontiers. Drawn by Shalom Schotten

41 Marble table top showing map of France, 1684. Musée de Versailles. Photo: Service de Documentation photographique de la Réunion des Musées Nationaux

42 *Le Camp de Coudun près de Compiègne ou l'Art de la Guerre enseigné par le Roy à Messeigneurs les Princes Enfants de France.* Anonymous engraving. B.N., Paris

43 *Ludovico XIV Regnante et Aedificante.* Medal. B.N., Paris. Photo: Giraudon

44 *Don Luis de Haro à l'Ile des Faisans.* Anonymous portrait. Musée Condé, Chantilly

46/47 Gobelin tapestry (of the second series, *Histoire de Louis XIV*) depicting the meeting of Louis XIV and Philip IV, 7 June 1660, on the Ile des Faisans. Photo: Giraudon

48 Maria Teresa in middle age. Marble relief c. 1680 attributed to Coysevox for the Crypt of the Basilica at St Denis, Paris. Photo: Giraudon

49 *La Chasse Royale de Chambor.* Anonymous engraving. B.N., Paris. Photo: Viollet

50 Portrait of Louise de La Vallière as Diana, c. 1661, probably by Joseph Werner (1637-1710). Musée de Versailles. Photo: Giraudon

51 Sculpture in the grounds of Versailles. Photo: Giraudon

52 *La France Galante, Estampe Allégorique sur les Amours du Roy.* Engraving of 1731 by Bernard Picart (1673-1733) remounted and captioned 'Année 1661'. B.N., Paris

53 Madame de Montespan with four of her children. Painting after P. Mignard. Musée de Versailles

54 Louis XIV (1668). Engraving (second state) by Robert Nanteuil. B.N., Paris. Photo: Giraudon
Louis XIV (1676). Engraving by Robert Nanteuil. B.N., Paris. Photo Giraudon

55 Françoise d'Aubigné, marquise de Maintenon, as her patron saint, Francisca Romana. Portrait c.

1694, by Pierre Mignard. Louvre. Photo: Giraudon

56 The duc de Guise at the carousel of 5 June 1662 in a costume designed by Henri de Gissey. Engraving by Silvestre after Jacques Bailly (1629-c. 1679). Musée de Versailles. Photo: Giraudon

57 *Enfant et Dauphin.* Sketch by Puget, 1651. Ecole des Beaux-Arts, Paris. Photo: Giraudon
Putto. Detail of bronze vase by Claude Ballin (1615-78) in the park of Versailles. Photo: Giraudon

58 Louis XIV in middle age. Marble bust, 1679-80, by Coysevox. Musée de Versailles. Photo: Giraudon
The Dauphin as a young man. Marble bust, 1679-80, by Coysevox. Musée de Versailles. Photo: Giraudon

59 Louis-Auguste, duc de Maine. Engraving by M. Dossier (1684-1750) after Rigaud. B.N., Paris. Photo: Giraudon
Louis-Alexandre, comte de Toulouse. Anonymous portrait. Musée Condé, Chantilly. Photo: Giraudon

60 *La Maison Royale de France.* Engraving c. 1705 by Henri Bonnart (1642-1711). B.N., Paris
Marie-Adélaïde of Savoy as Diana. Sculpture, 1710, by Coysevox. Louvre. Photo: Giraudon

61 *Louis XIV assistant à une leçon donnée au Dauphin,* c. 1715. Anonymous painting. Musée Carnavalet, Paris. Photo: Viollet

63 J. B. Colbert, 1667. Anonymous portrait. Musée de Versailles. Photo: Giraudon
Portrait of Louvois by Pierre Mignard. Rheims. Photo: Giraudon
Portrait of Torcy. Engraving by M. Dossier after Rigaud. B.N., Paris

65 *L'auguste Procession de la Chasse de Ste Geneviève, en l'Eglise de Notre Dame,* 16 May 1709. Anonymous engraving. B.N., Paris

66 Portrait of Vauban by Le Brun. Bibliothèque du Génie, Paris. Photo: Giraudon
Plan of Vauban's fortifications at Lille. Engraving presented to Prince Eugène of Savoy by E. H. Fricx, a Brussels publisher, in 1709. British Museum, Map Room, Maps 28 e 20
Study, c. 1709, of a guardsman by Antoine Watteau. Musée Condé, Chantilly. Photo: Giraudon

67 *Armée Française.* Anonymous engraving. B.N., Paris. Photo: Viollet

68 Louis XIV. Painting by Adam Frans van der Meulen (1632–90). Photo: Giraudon

69 *Le Passage du Rhin*, 1672. Anonymous engraving. B.N., Paris

70 *Marseille. Representation de la Marine Marchande.* Anonymous painting. Photo: Giraudon
Man of war. Study by Le Brun. Louvre. Photo: Giraudon

71 *Le S^r. Jean Baert Capitaine de Vaisseau.* Engraving by Antoine Trouvain (1656–1718). B.N., Paris

72 Obverse and reverse of commemorative medal, 1699, by Jean Mauger (d. 1722) inscribed 'Securitas Alsatiae'. Collection of the author. Photo: Ray Gardner

73 *Etablissement de l'Académie des Sciences*, detail from a painting, c. 1667, by Henri Testelin (1616–95). Musée de Versailles. Photo: Giraudon

75 Fortress of Pignerol. Detail of anonymous engraving. Collection Lallemant de Betz. B.N., Paris

77 *Entrée de Louis XIV et de la Reine Marie-Thérèse à Douai*, 2–3 August 1667. Engraving after a painting by Van der Meulen. Photo: Viollet

78 *La Holande malade.* Anonymous engraving. B.N., Paris
Franse Druck-Pers. Gestelt in Hollant 1672 en 1673. Anonymous engraving. B.N., Paris

79 *Le jeu de l'hombre des princes de l'Europe.* Anonymous engraving. B.N., Paris

83 Vase, *Secours de Hongrie* (also called *Vase de la Guerre*), by Coysevox, 1684–85, still *in situ* in the grounds at Versailles. Photo: Giraudon

89 *Le Doge de Gênes présente ses excuses à Versailles*, 1685, by Le Brun. Musée de Versailles. Photo: Giraudon

90 *Lotterie Royale.* Anonymous engraving, 1675. B.N., Paris
Sixième chambre des apartements. Engraving, 1694, by Antoine Trouvain. B.N., Paris. Photo: Viollet

91 *Le Buffet* (exhibited 1728), painting by Jean-Baptiste Chardin (1699–1779), showing in accurate detail one of the silver dishes used by Louis for the 'appartements'. Louvre. Photo: Giraudon

92 Jean Racine. Engraving by G. Edelinck (1640–1707) after Santerre (1651–1717). From E. Bourgeois, *Le Grand Siècle* (Paris 1896)
Nicolas Boileau-Despréaux. Portrait by Rigaud. Dulwich College Picture Gallery. Photo: Mansell Collection, London

93 *Attaque contre les Jésuites. Opposition entre leur richesse et leurs 'méfaits' et la pauvreté des Frères mineurs.* Anonymous seventeenth-century engraving. Photo: Viollet

94 *Ludovico Magno.* Engraving, 1686, by Elias Hainzelman (1640–93). B.N., Paris. Photo: Viollet

95 *La Cérémonie du Mariage de Monseig.^r le Duc de Bourgogne avec Madame la Princesse Marie-Adelaide de Savoye*, 7 December 1697. Engraving, 1697, by R. Bonnart. B.N., Paris

96 Allegorical painting, c. 1669, of Louis XIV and his family by J. Nocret (1615–72), painted for Philippe I, duc d'Orléans, for Saint-Cloud. Musée de Versailles. Photo: Bulloz

97 The marquis de Dangeau in his robes as Grand Master of the Order of St Lazare. Anonymous engraving after a painting of 1702 by Rigaud. Photo: Giraudon
Le château de Marly du côté des Jardins. Engraving by Jean Langlois. Photo: Giraudon

98 *Fontaine d'Amphitritte*, Marly. Design, unsigned. Archives Nationales. Photo: Giraudon
Vase de fleurs sur un Tapis Bleu. Anonymous painting. Musée Tesse, Le Mans. Photo: Giraudon

99 The Salle des Gardes de la Reine, 1679–81, Versailles, by Le Brun. Photo: Giraudon
Le Mois Février, one of a series of twelve engravings by Le Brun. Photo: Giraudon

100 Louis dancing in a ballet. Anonymous print, 1665. Photo: Viollet
The chariot of Apollo by Tuby in the park of Versailles. Photo: Giraudon

101 *Vue et Perspective de Château de Versailles côté jardin.* Engraving, 1680, by Aveline. B.N., Paris. Photo: Viollet
Detail of symbolic figure of Sâone river (undated) by Tuby in the park of Versailles. Photo: Giraudon

102 Details showing nymph and *putto* from the balustrade of the Bassin de Diane, 1690, by Le Hongre in the park of Versailles. Photo: Viollet
Vénus accroupie or *Vénus honteuse*, 1686, by Coysevox. Marble, Louvre. Photo: Viollet

103 Caryatid supporting the porch, Hôtel de Ville, Toulon. Sculpture by Puget, 1656. Musée de Sculpture Comparée. Photo: Viollet
Milo of Crotona, sculpture by Puget, 1671–82, placed in the park of Versailles, 1683. Louvre. Photo: Viollet
La Garonne. Sculpture, 1685–86, by Coysevox. Musée de Versailles. Photo: Viollet

104 Portrait of Louis XIV. Anonymous. Musée Condé, Chantilly. Photo: Giraudon
Louis XIV on horseback. Sketch attributed to Puget. Musée des Beaux-Arts, Marseilles. Photo: Giraudon

105 *Sur la porte du Palais du Cardinal Porto-Carrero.* Anonymous engraving. B.N., Paris

106 *Recrues allant joindre le regiment en 1709.* Painting after Watteau.

INDEX Page numbers in *italic* type refer to illustrations. * indicates footnote.